SPURGEON'S VERSE EXPOSITION ON ROMANS

By Charles H. Spurgeon

ISBN: 9781520322650

January 2017

Charles H. Spurgeon's Romans Commentary Contents

FOREWORD

Charles Haddon Spurgeon (1834-92) is known as the Prince of Preachers because of his extraordinary gift as a preacher of God's word. His ability was God-given and he used it for the glory of his Lord.

He gave his heart and life to Christ at the age of 15 after being forced to seek shelter from a snow storm in a Methodist chapel. Spurgeon was only 19 when he was called into full-time ministry as pastor of New Park Street Chapel. This Church, of course, eventually grew through God's grace which necessitated it moving to newly built premises and took the new name of the Metropolitan Tabernacle.

Spurgeon is most often remembered as being a preacher with little emphasis placed on other areas of his ministry. He was responsible for facilitating the opening of an orphanage, a college for training pastors and greatly supported the selling of Christian books. His ministry was anything but one-sided!

What we should remember is that Spurgeon communicated God's word and he was happy to use any medium that was available to him. His written works were invaluable as they were available to the many people who were unable to hear him preach. Indeed his volume, "Lectures To My Students" was published and as well as general sale copies were provided to many ministers around the country at their request and at the expense of Susannah Spurgeon who administered a fund to facilitate this generosity.

This book you are holding is not the product of Spurgeon's writing ministry nor the result of his preaching. These words are all Spurgeon's and they came about as the result of him expounding a chapter of the Bible during his Sunday service. Such was his gift that he could do this with very little specific preparation. He would select a chapter and tell the congregation the salient points and matters contained therein.

It is not a complete commentary of Scripture, indeed many chapters of the Bible did not receive this attention from him. Indeed in this commentary on Ephesians he had not provided an exegesis on chapter 4. But what Spurgeon left was a legacy of inspired, accurate and valuable insights into Scripture. These words you will read are for the preacher but, and more importantly, they are for every Christian. We pray that you will find that they help open Scripture to you in a new way.

We make use of commentaries, lexicons and concordances to help us better understand God's word. But these tools must never supplant or replace the Bible. There is no substitute to reading His word in order that we might apply it to our own lives.

Every blessing in the name of our Lord, Jesus Christ.

ROMANS 1

Verses 1-17

Romans 1:1. Paul, a servant of Jesus Christ, called to be an apostle, separated unto the gospel of God,

Paul has many titles, and he delights to mention them in writing to these Christians at Rome. He puts first his highest title: "A servant of Jesus Christ." He glories in being a servant of the crucified Christ, a servant of him who was despised and rejected of men; so do we. Paul was called out from among men, effectually "called" of God "to be an apostle, separated" — set apart — "unto the gospel of God." He believed that he was separated for that purpose at his birth; but he was specially "separated unto the gospel of God" on the road to Damascus. It is a happy thing when a minister feels that he has nothing to do with anything else but the gospel; that commands all his thought, all his talent, all his time.

Romans 1:2. (Which he had promised afore by his prophets in the holy scriptures,)

All the gospel is in the Old Testament as well as in the New, for the gospel which Paul was called to preach was promised afore by the prophets in the Holy Scriptures.

Romans 1:3-4. Concerning his Son Jesus Christ our Lord, which was made of the seed of David according to the flesh; and declared to be the Son of God with power, according to the spirit of holiness, by the resurrection from the dead:

He is as much the Son of God as he was the Son of man. The humanity is as true as the divinity, the divinity as true as the humanity.

Romans 1:5. BY whom we have received grace and apostleship, for obedience to the faith among all nations, for his name:

Paul felt that he was sent to preach among all the, Gentiles. He had a large bishopric; James might keep to the Jews, but Paul's diocese included every land, he was to preach "among all nations."

Romans 1:6-7. Among whom are ye also the called of Jesus Christ: to all that be in Rome, beloved of God, called to be saints: Grace to you and peace from God our Father, and the Lord Jesus Christ.

The gospel is good news; and the man who has to preach it is full of good wishes. He wishes the best possible things to everybody with whom he comes in contact: "Grace to you and peace from God our Father, and the Lord Jesus Christ."

Romans 1:8. First, I thank my God through Jesus Christ for you all, that your faith is spoken of throughout the whole world.

Oh, I would it were so with us, that we had faith that could be spoken of throughout the whole world! I am afraid that some have none to speak of; these saints in Rome had such faith that the noise thereof went abroad everywhere, and all people wondered at them.

Romans 1:9. For God is my witness, whom I serve with my spirit in the gospel of his Son, that without ceasing I make mention of you always in my prayers;

No wonder that they prospered so well when Paul always made mention of them in his prayers. Some churches would prosper better if some of you remembered them more in prayer. Of course, you all pray for the church of which you are members; could you not set aside in your heart a little space for some poor church that is dwindling down to nothing? Could you not pray it up again? Who knows what blessing would come upon pastor and people if you bore them on your hearts?

Romans 1:10. Making request, if by any means now at length I might have a prosperous journey by the will of God to come unto you.

Paul prayed about that matter, and we may pray about our journeys. I like to hear the old-fashioned expression, "Be pleased, O Lord, to grant journeying mercies," for there are such things; and when the servants of God are going about, with a view to spread the gospel, we ought to pray that they may travel in safety.

Romans 1:11. For I long to see, you, that I may impart unto you some spiritual gift, to the end ye may be established;

He wanted to go to Rome because he felt that he would take something with him. He was a poor man, so he could not take any golden or silvern gifts; but he was a chosen mail, so he believed that he could impart unto them some spiritual gift. Oh, what a largess does a man of God distribute when his Lord is with him! I do pray tonight that, feeble as I am, and unqualified as I am to bless you, yet even this night all of you who are the people of God may get some spiritual gift. I do not know what you want; but our heavenly Father does. May every one of you get, distinctly from his right hand, some spiritual gift to the end that you may be established, that you may get good root-hold, that you may be firmly fixed on the sure foundation!

Romans 1:12-13. That is, that I may he comforted together with you by the mutual faith both of you and me. Now I would not have you ignorant, brethren, that oftentimes I purposed to come unto you, (but was let hitherto,) that I might have some fruit among you also, even as among other Gentiles.

Rome was a sink of iniquity; it was the den of the lions, where Nero was, who would speedily devour, like a lion, the minister of Christ. Paul wanted somehow to get into that old city on the seven bills, and to pluck some fruit for God even from the vine that was planted there; but he was hindered.

Romans 1:14-15. I am debtor both to the Greeks, and to the Barbarians; both to the wise, and to the unwise. So, as much as in me is, I am ready to preach the gospel to you that are at Rome also.

I do not suppose that Paul guessed that he would be sent there at the government expense, but he was. The Roman Empire had to find a ship for him, and a fit escort for him, too; and he entered the city as an ambassador in bonds. When our hearts are set on a thing, and we pray for it, God may grant us the blessing; but, it may be, in a way that we never looked for. You shall go to Rome, Paul; but you shall go in chains. He had not thought of that plan; still, it was the best way in which he could go. I do not know how he could have preached to the Emperor except as a prisoner; but when he was brought before him to be tried, then he had an opportunity of speaking even to the brutal creature who was called the Emperor of Rome.

Romans 1:16-17. For I am not ashamed of the gospel of Christ: for it is the power of God unto salvation to every one that believeth; to the Jew first, and also to the Greek. For therein is the righteousness of God revealed from faith to faith: as it is written, The just shall live by faith.

That is the sum and substance of the gospel: "The just shall live by faith." The law is, "He that doeth these things shall live by them;" but the gospel is, "The just shall live by faith." "Wherefore, being justified by faith, we have peace with God." The Lord give to us all that saving faith, for Christ's sake! Amen.

Verses 1-25

Romans 1:1-2. Paul, a servant of Jesus Christ, called to be an apostle, separated unto the gospel of God. (Which he had promised afore by his prophets in the holy scriptures.)

Paul had not seen the Romans when he wrote this epistle. They were strangers to him, and therefore he begins by asserting his apostleship. "called to be an apostle, separated unto the gospel of God." That expression should be true of every Christian minister. We are not apostles; but we are "separated unto the gospel of God." I do not think that we are called to have anything to do with party politics, or social problems, or any such questions; we are set apart for this purpose. "separated unto the gospel of God." There are plenty of people who can attend to those things better than we can/ If we mind our own business, or rather, if we mind our Master's business, we who are ministers will have quite enough to do. "Separated unto the gospel of God." There are some brethren who in preaching are as timid as mice; but on a political platform they can roar like lions. Had not they better take to what they like best, and give up the work at which they are not at home? For my part, I believe that I am like Paul when he says that he was "separated unto the gospel of God." I am set apart unto the gospel, cut off from everything else that I may preach the glorious gospel of the blessed God to the perishing sons of men. (Which he had promised afore by his prophets in the holy scriptures.) Notice, brethren, how reverent the apostles were to Holy Scripture. They had no doubt about its inspiration. They quoted the old Testament, and delighted to make it a kind of basis for the New Testament: "which he had promised afore by his prophets in the Holy Scriptures."

Romans 1:3-4. Concerning his Son Jesus Christ our Lord, which was made the seed of David according to the flesh; and declared to be the Son of God with power, according to the spirit of holiness, by the resurrection from the dead:

What a glorious Lord we serve! He is God's Son: "Jesus Christ our Lord." In his human nature, he is a Man of royal race: "of the seed of David." He was a man, therefore he died: but he rose again, for he was more than man:
"declared to be the Son of God with power."

Romans 1:5-6. By whom we have received grace and apostleship, for obedience to the faith among all notions, for his name: among whom are ye also the called of Jesus Christ:

That is a sweet name for every truly converted man. "called of Jesus Christ." He has called you personally, he has called you effectually, he has called you out of the world, he has called you into fellowship with himself: "the called of Jesus Christ." The revised version has it: "call to be Jesus Christ's." those who are called by Christ, are called to be his.

Romans 1:7-8. To all that be in Rome, beloved of God, called to be saints: Grace to you and peace from God our Father, and the Lord Jesus Christ. First, I thank my God through Jesus Christ for you all, that your faith is spoken of throughout the whole world.

What contrasts we have in the seventh verse! "In Rome, beloved of God." "In Rome called to be saints." God has beloved ones in the darkest parts of the earth. There is all the more reason for them to be saints because they are surrounded by sinners. They must have had true faith, or they could not have confessed Christ between the jaws of a lion, for they lived in Rome, with Nero hunting after Christians, as if they had been wild beasts, and yet they were not ashamed of the gospel of Christ.

Romans 1:9. For God is my witness, whom I serve with my spirit in the gospel of his Son, that without ceasing I make mention of you always in my prayers;

This man, Paul, did a great deal by prayer. I remember a minister, who is now with the Lord, who was thanked by his people for his wonderful sermons; but he said to them, "You never thanked me for my prayers, yet they were the best part of my service for you." When men of God are mighty in prayer, we owe much to them.

Romans 1:10. Making request, if by any means now at length I might have a prosperous journey by the will of God to come unto you.

Paul wanted to go to Rome; but I do not suppose that he ever thought that he would go there at the expense of the government, with an imperial guard to take care of him all the way. We pray, and God gives us the answer to our petitions; but often in a way of which we should never have dreamed. Paul goes to Rome as a prisoner for Christ's sake. Now suppose Paul had gone to Rome in any other capacity, he could not have seen Caesar, he could not have obtained admission into Caesar's house. The prison of the Palatine was just under the vast palace of the Caesars; and everybody in the house could come into the guard-room. And have a talk with Paul if they were minded so to do. I suppose that, whatever I might be willing to pay, I could not have preached in the palace of the Queen, even in this nominally Christian country; but Paul was installed as a royal chaplain over Caesar's household in the guard-room of the Palatine prison.

How wonderfully God works to accomplish his divine purposes!

Romans 1:11-12. For I long to see you, that I may impart unto you some spiritual gift, to the end ye may be established; that is, that I may be comforted together with you by the mutual faith both of you and me.

Paul wanted his faith to establish theirs, and their faith to establish his. Christians grow rich by and exchange of spiritual commodities; and I am afraid some Christians are very poor because they do not engage in the spiritual bartering with one another. You know how it was in the old time, "They that feared the Lord spake often one to another." Shall I tell you how it is now? They that fear not the Lord speak often one against another. That is a very sad difference. Oh, for more Christian communion; for when we blend our "mutual faith:, we are "comforted together"; each believer grows stronger as he cheers his brother in the Lord!

Romans 1:13. Now I would not have you ignorant, brethren, that oftentimes I purposed to come unto you, (but was let hitherto,) that I might have some fruit among you also, even as among other Gentiles.

Ah! Paul, you could not go when you wished. Caesar must convoy you. Your Master would have you go to Rome under the protection of the eagles of your empire. God has servants everywhere: he can make Satan himself provide the body-guard for his faithful apostle's journey.

Romans 1:14. I am a debtor both to the Greeks, and to the Barbarians; both to the wise, and to the unwise.

Paul felt a debt to everybody. The God who saved him, had saved him that he might preach the gospel in every place he could reach. Brethren, if you have received much from God, you are so much the debtor to men; and you are debtors not only to the respectable, but to the disreputable, debtors not only to those who come to a place of worship, but to the dwellers in the slums, "to the Greeks, and to the barbarians; to the wise and to the unwise."

Romans 1:15-16. So, as much as in me is, I am ready to preach the gospel to you that are at Rome also. For I am not ashamed of the gospel of Christ:

Many other people were ashamed of the gospel of Christ. It was too simple; it had not enough of mystery about it; it had not enough of worldly wisdom about it. Paul says, "I am not ashamed of the gospel of Christ," and then gives his reason for not being ashamed of it, —

Romans 1:16-17. For it is the power of God unto salvation to every one that believeth; to the Jew first, and also to the Greek. For therein is the righteousness of God revealed from faith to faith: as it is written, The just shall live by faith.

The gospel tells us about this living by faith, this believing, this receiving righteousness through believing, and not through working. This is the sweet story of the cross, of which Paul was not ashamed.

Romans 1:18. For the wrath of God is revealed from heaven against all ungodliness and unrighteousness of men, who hold the truth in unrighteousness;

Those last words may be read, "Who hold down the truth in unrighteousness." They will not let the truth work upon their hearts; they will not allow it to operate in their minds; but they try to make it an excuse for their sin. Is there anybody here who is holding down the truth to prevent its entering his heart? I fear that there are some such persons, who have come here for years, and the truth has pricked them, troubled them, made them lie awake at night; but they are holding it down, like one who grasps a wild animal by the ears, and holds it down for fear it should bite him. Oh, sirs, when you are afraid of the truth, you may be well be afraid of hell! When you and the truth quarrel, you had better end your fighting soon, for you will have the worst of it if you do not yield: "For the wrath of God is revealed from heaven against all ungodliness and unrighteousness of men, who hold down the truth in unrighteousness."

Romans 1:19-20. Because that which may be known of God is manifest in them; for God hath shewed it unto them. For the invisible things of him from the creation of the world are clearly seen, being understood by the things that are made, even his eternal power and Godhead; so that they are without excuse:

Men who never heard the gospel can see God in his works if they open their eyes. There is written upon the face of nature enough to condemn men if they do not turn to God. There is a gospel of the sea, and of the heavens, of the stars, and of the sun; and if men will not read it, they are guilty, for they are willfully ignorant of what they might know, and ought to know.

Romans 1:21-22. Because that, when they knew God, they glorified him not as God, neither were thankful; but became vain in their imaginations, and their foolish heart was darkened. Professing themselves to be wise, they became fools,

The way to be a fool is to pretend to be wise. A short cut to wisdom is the confession of folly. The near way to folly is the profession of wisdom.

Romans 1:23-24. And changed the glory of the uncorruptible God into an image made like to corruptible man, and to birds, and fourfooted beasts, and creeping things. Wherefore God also gave them up to uncleanness through the lust of their own hearts, to dishonour their own bodies between themselves:

It is very easy to make a beast of yourself when you have made a beast to be your god, as the Egyptians did, when they worshipped the god that they had made in the form of an ox, or a crocodile, or a cat.

Romans 1:25. Who changed the truth of God into a lie, and worshipped and served the creature more than the Creator, who is blessed for ever. Amen.

There are many preachers who have "changed the truth of God into a lie"; and by their exaltation of man, they have "worshipped and served the creature more than the Creator, who is blessed for ever." God save all of us from such idolatry as that! Amen.

ROMANS 2

Verses 25-29

Romans 2:25. For circumcision verily profiteth, if thou keep the law: but if thou be a breaker of the law, thy circumcision is made uncircumcision.

Paul is dealing with the Jew, who was apt to think that he must have a preference beyond the Gentiles on account of his circumcision.

Romans 2:26-29. Therefore if the uncircumcision keep the righteousness of the law, shall not his uncircumcision be counted for circumcision? And shall not uncircumcision which is by nature if it fulfill the law, judge thee, who by the letter and circumcision dost transgress the law? For he is not a Jew, which is one outwardly; neither is that circumcision, which is outward in the flesh: But he is a Jew, which is one inwardly; and circumcision is that of the heart, in the spirit, and not in the letter; whose praise is not of men, but of God.

If this principle were fully recognized everywhere, it would certainly put an end to all that notion of sacramentarianism which some men hold. It is not the outward, not the external, not the form and ceremony; it is the inward work of the spirit; it is holiness and change of heart. Let none of us ever fall into the gross error of those who imagine that there is attached to certain ceremonies a certain degree of grace. It is not so. He is not a Christian which is one outwardly, he is a Christian who is one inwardly.

This exposition consisted of readings from Psalms 110; Romans 2:25-29; Romans 3.

ROMANS 3

Verses 1-31

Romans 3:1-2. What advantage then hath the Jew? or what profit is there of circumcision? Much every way: chiefly, because that unto them were committed the oracles of God.

It was a great thing to be a Jew in those old times. When all the rest of the world was in the dark, the Jews had the light: "Unto them were committed the oracles of God."

Romans 3:3. For what if some did not believe? shall their unbelief make the faith of God without effect?

That is to say, if they did not believe God, did that make him untrue?

Romans 3:4. God forbid: yea, let God be true, but every man a liar; as it is written, That thou mightest be justified in thy sayings, and mightest overcome when thou art judged.

Whatever men did under the old law, however faithless they might be. God was true and faithful still.

Romans 3:5-6. But if our unrighteousness commend the righteousness of God, what shall we say? Is God unrighteous who taketh vengeance? (I speak as a man) God forbid: for then how shall God judge the world?

Whenever anybody insinuates that God is not just, Paul protests against such an idea. "No," says he, "he must of necessity be just because he is God; for how could he judge the world if he were unrighteous?"

Romans 3:7-8. For if the truth of God hath more abounded through my lie unto his glory, why yet am I also judged as a sinner? And not rather, (as we be slanderously reported, and as some affirm that we say,) Let us do evil, that good may come? whose damnation is just.

No Christian man ever did say, "Let us do evil that good may come." If anybody else ever does say it, his condemnation is most just. Albeit that God, in infinite wisdom, does cause even the sin of man to illustrate the greatness of his grace, yet that by no means excuses his sin, but leaves it an abominable evil, most hateful in the sight of the thrice-holy Jehovah.

Romans 3:9. What then? are we better than they? No, in no wise: for we have before proved both Jews and Gentiles, that they are all under sin;

Read the earlier chapters of this Epistle, chapters that are enough to make the heart sick to read them, and to make the head ache with the memory of them, and when you have read them, you will say that Paul has proved that both Jews and Gentiles are under sin.

Romans 3:10. As it is written, There is none righteous, no, not one:

Note in the passage we are going to read how Paul rings the changes upon those two words, "All" and "none." He begins with the word "none."

Romans 3:11-12. There is none that understandeth, there is none that seeketh after God. They are all gone out of the way, they are together become unprofitable; there is none that doeth good, no, not one.

Yet men come and talk to us about the righteous heathen whose virtues they extol, the imaginary good people, for there are none such actually in existence. Here the Lord himself is speaking, and the Spirit of God is quoting from passages of the Old Testament, which he puts together to describe the character of humanity. How sweeping are all the terms! "There is none righteous, no, not one. There is none that understandeth, there is none that seeketh after God. They are all gone out of the way, they are together become unprofitable; there is none that doeth good, no, not one."

Romans 3:13-16. Their throat is an open sepulcher, with their tongues they have used deceit, the poison of asps is under their lips: whose mouth is full of cursing and bitterness: their feet are swift to shed blood: destruction and misery are in their ways:

How true that last verse is of many today! Their sins are destroying them, the lusts of the flesh destroy the body, drunkenness and such like sin are destructive habits, and they make those who practice them to be miserable: "Destruction and misery are in their ways." What miserable persons, what miserable families, what miserable countries, are made by indulgence in sin! There is no true happiness without holiness.

Romans 3:17. And the way of peace have they not known:

Quietness, happiness, and rest are not known by sinful men. They are not in the way of finding peace.

Romans 3:18. There is no fear of God before their eyes,

How true is this terrible accusation, especially of this present age! Men seem to be casting off all fear of God. Anyone who reads human history will, I think, detect that the present condition of society in our country, religiously, is wonderfully like the condition of France before the great Revolution, which brought so much bloodshed with it. Everything seems loosening, and broadening, and tending downwards; and especially "there is no fear of God before their eyes."

Romans 3:19. Now we know that what things soever the law saith, it saith to them who are under the law: that every mouth may be stopped, and all, the world may become guilty before God.

Every man by nature tries to open his mouth, and say the best he can for himself, but it is the object of God's law to shut every man's mouth; and when we come to that condition, then there is hope for us. When we have nothing to say for ourselves, then the Lord Jesus will open his mouth for the dumb, and plead for the guilty in the courts of God.

Romans 3:20. Therefore by the deeds of the law there shall no flesh be justified in his sight: for by the law is the knowledge of sin,

All the law can do is to show us our sin. The law is a mirror, and looking in it you can see your spots; but you cannot wash in a looking-glass. If you want to be cleansed from your stains, you must go somewhere else. The object of the law of God is not to cleanse us, but to show us how much cleansing we need; to reveal our disease, not to find a remedy for it.

Romans 3:21-22. But now the righteousness of God without the law is manifested, being witnessed by the law and the prophets; even the righteousness of God which is by faith of Jesus Christ unto all and upon all them that believe:

You see, we cannot become righteous by the law. Paul says that there is no one who has ever obtained righteousness in that way. We, on the contrary, have so sinned that we never can become righteous through the law; but there is a new way of righteousness, the way of the righteousness of God; and God's righteousness is much better than the best human righteousness can ever be conceived to be. There is a righteousness which comes to us by faith in Jesus Christ, not by doing, but by believing, a righteousness which is freely bestowed upon all them that believe.

Romans 3:22-24. For there is no difference: for all have sinned, and come short of the glory of God; being justified freely by his grace through the redemption that is in Christ Jesus:

I have heard persons ask, "Why do you say, 'free grace'? If it is grace, it must be free." Well, we say "free grace", because the Scripture says, "freely by his grace"; and as the Lord never uses superfluous words, we conceive that we are not guilty of tautology when we say "free grace,"

Romans 3:25-26. Whom God hath set forth to be a propitiation through faith in his blood, to declare his righteousness for the remission of sins that are past, through the forbearance of God, to declare, I say, at this time his righteousness: that he might be just, and the justifier of him which believeth in Jesus.

Not of him who works for salvation, but of him who believes; not of him who merits, but of him who trusts. This is God's way of righteousness, and we are sent to declare it. Oh, that the Spirit of God may be given to make the declaration acceptable to your hearts!

Romans 3:27. Where is boasting then? It is excluded.

Shut out, done with.

Romans 3:27. By what law? of works?

No, no, the law of works would have allowed us to boast. We should have merited whatever we earned by our own excellence, and we might have gloried in it.

Romans 3:27-31. Nay: but by the law of faith. Therefore we conclude that a man is justified by faith without the deeds of the law. Is he the God of the Jews only? is he not also of the Gentiles? Yea, of the Gentiles also: seeing it is one God, which shall justify the circumcision by faith, and uncircumcision through faith. Do we then make void the law through faith? God forbid: yea, we establish the law.

This exposition consisted of readings from Romans 3, and Romans 4:16-25.

Verses 9-27

Romans 3:9. What then? are we better than they?

The first chapter of the Epistle to the Romans contains so horrible an account of the manners of the Gentiles, the heathen of Paul's day, that it is one of the most painful chapters in Scripture to read. Not long ago, one of our missionaries, out in China, was attacked concerning the Bible on this very ground. One of the learned men said to him, "This Bible of yours cannot be as ancient as you say that it is, for it is quite clear that the next chapter of the Epistle to the Nomads must have been written by somebody who had been in China, and who had seen the habits and ways of the people here," — so accurate is the Holy Spirit, who knew right well what the ways and manners and secret vices of the heathen were, and still are. But the Jews said, "Ah, but this is a description of the Gentiles." So Paul replies, "What then? are we better than they?

Romans 3:9-10. No, in no wise: for we have before proved both Jews and Gentile, that they are all under sin; as it is written, There is none righteous, no, not one:

Then he selects passages out of different parts of Scripture to show what man is by nature.

Romans 3:11-18. There is none that understandeth, there is none that seeketh after God. They are all gone out of the way, they are together become unprofitable; there is none that doeth good, no, not one. Their throat is an open sepulcher, with their tongues they have used deceit; the poison of asps is under their lips: whose mouth is full of cursing and bitterness: their feet are swift to shed blood: destruction and misery are in their ways: and the way of peace have they not known: there is no fear of God before their eyes.

These are all quotations from Old Testament Scriptures, from their own psalmists and prophets, from whom Paul quotes to the Jews so that they might see what their own character was by nature.

23

Romans 3:19. Now we know that what things soever the law saith, it saith to them who are under the law: that every mouth may be stopped, and all the world may become guilty before God.

The law was given to the Jews, and the descriptions which it gives must be descriptions of the Jews "Therefore," says Paul, "as Gentile mouths have been already stopped by the descriptions of their vices, you also, the favored people of God, have your mouths stopped by the descriptions of yourselves taken from your own prophets."

Romans 3:20. Therefore by the deeds of the law there shall no flesh —

Whether Jew or Gentile, —

Romans 3:20-21. Be justified in his sight: for by the law is the knowledge of sin. But now —

Since man is lost, since man is guilty, —

Romans 3:21-27. The righteousness of God without the law is manifested, being witnessed by the law and the prophets: even the righteousness of God which is by faith of Jesus Christ unto all and upon all them that believe: for there is no difference: for all have sinned, and come short of the glory of God; being justified freely by his grace through the redemption that is in Christ Jesus: whom God hath set forth to be a propitiation through faith in his blood, to declare his righteousness for the remission of sins that are past through the forbearance of God, to declare, I say, at this time his righteousness: that he might be just, and the justifier of him which believeth in Jesus. Where is boasting then?

If salvation is given to the guilty, and if all are guilty, — if no one can claim exemption, and yet salvation is freely given, — what then? Why, salvation must be purely by the grace of God; so let grace have all the honour. "Where is boasting then?"

Romans 3:27. It is excluded. By what law of works? Nay: but by the law of faith.

The law of works sometimes aids boasting, for a man rejoices and glories in what he has done; yet the law of works ought to stop our boasting because we are guilty in God's sight. The law of faith does stop our mouth, because we are under obligation to God, and do not dare to boast, seeing that we have nothing of good but what we have received from God.

This exposition consisted of readings from Romans 3:9-27; Romans 5:6-11; Romans 8:1-32.

Verses 9-31

Romans 3:9-18. What then? are we better than they? No, in no wise: for we have before proved both Jews and Gentiles, that they are all under sin; As it is written, There is none righteous, no, not one: There is none that understandeth, there is none that seeketh after God. They are all gone out of the way, they are together become unprofitable; there is none that doeth good, no, not one. Their throat is an open sepulcher: with their tongues they have used deceit; the poison of asps is under their lips: Whose mouth is full of cursing and bitterness: their feet are swift to shed blood.' Destruction and misery are in their ways: And the way ,of peace have they not known .' There is no fear of God before their eyes.

This is a description of man given 'by prophets in the olden times. "Now," says Paul, "we know that what things soever the law saith, it saith to them who are under the law." So that this is a description of the Jews, a description of the people who had the light, the best people that then were upon the face of the earth, and if these be the good people, where are the Gentiles, the bad ones, without the light?

Romans 3:19-22. Now we know that what things soever the law saith, it saith to them who ,are under the law; that every mouth may be stopped, and all the world may become guilty before God. Therefore by the deeds of the law there shall no flesh be justified in his sight: for by the law is the knowledge of sin. But now the righteousness of God without the law is manifested, being witnessed by the law and the prophets: Even the righteousness of God which is by faith of Jesus Christ unto ,all and upon all them that believe: for there is no difference:

There is no righteousness of works on the face of the earth. The law 'itself describes men as being sinful from their throat to their feet. Almost every member of the body is mentioned and described as being foul with sin. But, says Paul, there is another righteousness on the face of the earth, and that is the righteousness of God's grace, which comes through believing in Christ.

Romans 3:23-31. For all have sinned, and come short of the glory of God; Being justified freely by his grace through the redemption that is in Christ Jesus: Whom God hath set forth to be a propitiation through faith in his blood, to declare his righteousness for the remission of sins that are past, through the forbearance of God: To declare, I say, at this time his righteousness: that he might be just, and the justifier of him which believeth in Jesus Where is boasting then? It is excluded. By what law? of works? Nay: but by the law of faith. Therefore we conclude that a man is justified by faith without the deeds of the law. Is he the God of the Jews only? Is he not also of the Gentiles? Yes, of the Gentiles also: Seeing it is one God, which shall justify the circumcision by faith, and uncircumcision through faith. Do we then make void the law through faith? God forbid: yea, we establish the law.

Verses 19-31

Romans 3:19-20. Now we know that what things soever the law saith, it saith to them who are under the law: that every mouth may be stopped, and all the world may become guilty before God. Therefore by the deeds of the law there shall no flesh be justified in his sight: for by the law is the knowledge of sin.

The law can convict and condemn, but it can never justify the guilty. Its special work is to prove that they are not justified in sinning, and to stop their mouths from uttering any excuse for their sin.

Romans 3:21-24. But now the righteousness of God without the law is manifested, being witnessed by the law and the prophets; even the righteousness of God which is by faith of Jesus Christ unto all and upon all them that believe: for there is no difference: for all have sinned, and come short of the glory of God; being justified freely by his grace through the redemption that is in Christ Jesus:

Now there comes in a new principle, — the principle of grace, which accomplishes what the law never could accomplish; that is, the free justification of all the guilty ones who believe in Jesus. And this justification is a righteous one, seeing that it is based upon "the redemption that is in Christ Jesus:" —

Romans 3:25-27. Whom God hath set forth to be a propitiation through faith in his blood, to declare his righteousness for the remission of sins that are past, through the forbearance of God; to declare, I say, at this time his righteousness: that he might be just, and the justifier of him which believeth in Jesus. Where is boasting then? It is excluded. By what law? of works? Nay: but by the law of faith.

Faith's empty hand receives the free gift of grace, and that very fact excludes all boasting.

Romans 3:28-31. Therefore we conclude that a man is justified by faith without the deeds of the law. Is he the God of the Jews only? is he not also of the Gentiles? Yes, of the Gentiles also: seeing it is one God, which shall justify the circumcision by faith, and uncircumcision through faith. Do we then make void the law through faith? God forbid: yea, we establish the law.

This exposition consisted of readings from Romans 3:19-31; and Romans 4:1-21.

ROMANS 4

Verses 1-20

Romans 4:1-3. What shall we say then that Abraham our father, as pertaining to the flesh, hath found? For if Abraham were justified by works, he hath whereof to glory; but not before God. For what saith the scripture? Abraham believed God, and it was counted unto him for righteousness.

He stands as the great Father of believers, and this is the charter given to him, and given to all believers in him. "Abraham believed God, and it was counted to him for righteousness."

Romans 4:4. Now to him that worketh is the reward not reckoned of grace, but of debt.

That is to say, to him who hopes to be saved by his works, to whom salvation is of merit. He has worked for the reward. He has earned it. Do not talk about grace in that case.

Romans 4:5. But to him that worketh not, but believeth on him that justifieth the ungodly, his faith is counted for righteousness.

This is the man who does not go upon the line of works — who does not rest in his works at all, or bring them as a price to God. "His faith is counted for righteousness." It is a very wonderful thing that faith should stand in the stead of righteousness, and should make righteous all those that believe in God by Jesus Christ.

Romans 4:6-8. Even as David also describeth the blessedness of the man, unto whom God imputeth righteousness without works. Saying, Blessed are they whose iniquities are forgiven, and whose sins are covered. Blessed is the man to whom the Lord will not impute sin.

Instead of being a worker, this man had been an offender — a sinner. God did not impute it to him. He was a believer, and God imputed

31

righteousness to him on account of his faith, and did not impute sin to him. Then comes a very important inquiry.

Romans 4:9. Cometh this blessedness then upon the circumcision only, or upon the uncircumcision also?

Is circumcision so necessary that a man is justified by faith after he is circumcised, and could not be so justified if he were an uncircumcised man?

Romans 4:9-10. For we say that faith was reckoned to Abraham for righteousness.

How was it then reckoned? When he was in circumcision, or in uncircumcision? Look back to the history. See in what condition Abraham was when faith was reckoned to him for righteousness. Was it when he was in circumcision or in uncircumcision? The answer is: —

Romans 4:10-11. Not in circumcision, but in uncircumcision. And he received the sign of circumcision, a seal of the righteousness of the faith which he had yet being uncircumcised:

But the sign is to follow the thing signified. He is, first of all, justified by his faith, and then afterwards he receives the token of the covenant.

Romans 4:11. That he might be the father of all them that believe, though they be not circumcised: that righteousness might be imputed unto them also:

It is a very remarkable fact. A great many readers of the Book of Genesis would never have noticed it if the Holy Ghost had not called attention to the fact that father Abraham was justified by his faith before he was circumcised; and this is the reason of it — that he might be the father of all believers, whether they be circumcised or uncircumcised. "That righteousness might be imputed to them also."

Romans 4:12-13. And the father of circumcision to them who are not of the circumcision only, but who also walk in the steps of that faith of our father Abraham, which he had being yet uncircumcised. For the promise, that he should be the heir of the world, was not to Abraham, or to his seed, through the law, but through the righteousness of faith.

For the law was not even given when that covenant promise was made. The law was 400 years afterwards. The covenant of grace was the oldest covenant of all, and it shall stand fast, whatever shall happen.

Romans 4:14. For if they which are of the law be heirs, faith is made void, and the promise made of none effect:

If you are upon that tack of salvation by the law, then what have you to do with faith? And what have you to do with promise, and what have yea to do with Christ? You are on a different line altogether.

Romans 4:15. Because the law worketh wrath: for where no law is, there is no transgression.

That is plain enough. You cannot break a law if there is not any; and thus, through our sinfulness, the law becomes a cause of sin, and never does it become the cause of justification.

Romans 4:16. Therefore it is of faith, that it might be by grace:

Salvation is by faith alone, that it may be seen to be of the free favor of God, that we may not look to merit or look to human strength, but may look away to the abounding mercy of God in Christ Jesus.

Romans 4:16-17. To the end the promise might be sure to all the seed; not to that only which is of the law, but to that also which is of the faith of Abraham; who is the father of us all.

What a God we trust in — a God who quickeneth the dead. We have no faith unless we believe in such a God as this. We shall need such a God in order to bring us safely to his right hand at last.

Romans 4:18-20. Who against hope believed in hope, that he might become the father of many nations, according to that which was spoken, So shall thy seed be. And being not weak in faith, he considered not his own body now dead, when he was about an hundred years old, neither yet the deadness of Sarah's womb; He staggered not at the promise of God through unbelief; but was strong in faith, giving glory to God:

Men seem to think that only workers can give glory to God; but there is more glory given to God by one drachma of faith than by a ton of works. After all, works usually generate conceit and pride in us. But faith lays itself low before its God, and gives to him all the glory. God is never more glorified than he is by the believing confidence of his people when difficulties seem to come in the way. He was "strong in faith, giving glory to God."

Verses 1-21

Romans 4:1-8. What shall we say then that Abraham our father, as pertaining to the flesh, hath found? For if Abraham were justified by works, he hath whereof to glory; but not before God. For what saith the scripture? Abraham believed God, and it was counted unto him for righteousness. Now to him that worketh is the reward not reckoned of grace, but of debt. But to him that worketh not, but believeth on him that justifieth the ungodly, his faith is counted for righteousness. Even as David also describeth the blessedness of the man, unto whom God imputeth righteousness without works, saying, Blessed are they whose iniquities are forgiven, and whose sins are covered. Blessed is the man to whom the Lord will not impute sin.

There is a special blessedness, therefore, which comes to those who, by faith, are under the dispensation of grace. It came to Abraham, and it came to David; yet both Abraham and David were circumcised men belonging to a special race. So the question naturally arises, —

Romans 4:9-12. Cometh this blessedness then upon the circumcision only, or upon the uncircumcision also? for we say that faith was reckoned to Abraham for righteousness. How was it then reckoned? when he was in circumcision, or in uncircumcision? Not in circumcision, but in uncircumcision. And he received the sign of circumcision, a seal of the righteousness of the faith which he had yet being uncircumcised: that he might be the father of all them that believe, though they be not circumcised; that righteousness might be imputed unto them also: and the father of circumcision to them who are not of the circumcision only, but who also walk in the steps of that faith of our father Abraham, which he had being yet uncircumcised.

The historical argument is a very forcible one. The blessing was not given to Abraham as a circumcised man, but as a believing man; and hence it comes also to all of us who believe. What a mercy it is that there is, in this sense, no distinction between Jew and Gentile now! I hate that plan of reading the Scriptures in which we are told, when we lay hold of a gracious promise, "Oh, that is for the Jews." "Then I also am a Jew, for it is given to me." Every promise of God's Word belongeth to all those who have the faith to grasp it. We who have faith, are all in the covenant, and are thus the children of faithful Abraham; so be not afraid, ye who are the true seed, to take every blessing that belongs to your father Abraham and to all the seed.

Romans 4:13-14. For the promise, that he should be the heir of the world, was not to Abraham, or to his seed, through the law, but through the righteousness of faith. For if they which are of the law be heirs, faith is made void, and the promise made of none effect:

But that would also make void circumcision and the whole of the ancient covenant, seeing that the blessing was given to a man whom God had chosen before his circumcision, and before the ceremonial law had been promulgated.

Romans 4:15-17. Because the law worketh wrath: for where no law is, there is no transgression. Therefore it is of faith, that it might be by grace; to the end the promise might be sure to all the seed; not to that only which is of the law, but to that also which is of the faith of Abraham; who is the father of us all, (as it is written, I have made thee a father of many nations,)

Not a father of one select race of people only, but a father of all who, in any land, and speaking any language, are believers in the glorious Jehovah, who is the God of Abraham, and of Isaac, and of Jacob.

Romans 4:17. Before him whom he believed, even God, who quickeneth the dead, and calleth those things which be not as though they were.

Abraham was a believer in the God of resurrection, expecting to see Isaac raised up from the dead if he did actually offer him as a sacrifice to God. He was a believer in things that were not yet apparent to him, looking forward to them, and expecting to see them in due time;

believing in them because he believed in God, who "calleth those things which be not as though they were."

Romans 4:18-21. Who against hope believed in hope, that he might become the father of many nations, according to that which was spoken, So shall thy seed be. And being not weak in faith, he considered not his own body now dead, when he was about an hundred years old, neither yet the deadness of Sarah's womb: he staggered not at the promise of God through unbelief; but was strong in faith, giving glory to God; and being fully persuaded that, what he had promised, he was able also to perform.

This exposition consisted of readings from Romans 3:19-31; and Romans 4:1-21.

Verses 1-25

Romans 4:1. What shall we say then that Abraham our father as pertaining to the flesh, hath found?

What blessings did really come to Abraham, the father of the faithful? What is the nature of that covenant of grace which God made with him?

Romans 4:2. For if Abraham were justified by works, he hath whereof to glory; but not before God.

Certainly, before God, Abraham neither gloried nor yet was justified by his works.

Romans 4:3. For what saith the scripture?

That is the question for us always to ask, "What saith the Scripture?"

Romans 4:3. Abraham believed God, and it was counted unto him for righteousness.

There is no doubt about that point, for in Genesis 15:6 we read, "He believed in the Lord; and he counted it to him for righteousness."

Romans 4:4. Now to him that worketh is the reward not reckoned of grace, but of debt.

He gets what he earns, what he deserves to have, what he receives is "not reckoned of grace, but of debt."

Romans 4:5-8. But to him that worketh not, but believeth on him that justifieth the ungodly, his faith is counted for righteousness. Even as David also describeth the blessedness of the man, unto whom God imputeth righteousness without works, saying, Blessed are they whose iniquities are forgiven, and whose sins are covered. Blessed is the man to whom the Lord will not impute sin.

So then it seems that the blessings of salvation come to men through faith, and not through their own efforts,-not as the reward of merit, but as the simple gift of God's grace.

Romans 4:9. Cometh this blessedness then upon the circumcision only, or upon the uncircumcision also?

Is this blessing entailed upon the natural seed of Abraham alone, or is it for others besides the Jews?

Romans 4:9-10. For we say that faith was reckoned to Abraham for righteousness. How was it then reckoned? when he was in circumcision, or in uncircumcision? Not in circumcision, but in uncircumcision.

If you turn again to Genesis 15:6, and then to 17:10, you will find that Abraham was justified by faith before the rite of circumcision was instituted. The blessing came to him "not in circumcision, but in uncircumcision."

Romans 4:11-12. And he received the sign of circumcision, a seal of the righteousness of the faith which he had yet being uncircumcised: that he might be the father of all them that believe, though they be not circumcised; that righteousness might be imputed unto them also: and the father of circumcision to them who are not of the circumcision only, but who also walk in the steps of that faith of our father Abraham, which he had being yet uncircumcised.

The vital question is not, "How were we born?": or "What rites and ceremonies have been practiced upon us?" but, "Do we believe in God? Have we true faith in God's Word? Are we trusting our souls to the keeping of God's Son?"

Romans 4:13. For the promise, that he should be the heir of the world, was not to Abraham, or to his seed, through the law, but through the righteousness of faith.

The law was promulgated on mount Sinai four hundred years after the covenant of grace was made with Abraham the father of believers, and so made with all believers, for they are his true seed, and God has entered into a covenant of grace and salvation with them.

Romans 4:14-15. For if they which are of the law be heirs, faith is made void, and the promise made of none effect: because the law worketh wrath: for where no law is, there is no transgression.

So that the law is not for justification, but for condemnation. It is the law that reveals sin, and that shows sin to be sin; so men can never become right with God by the law.

Romans 4:16. Therefore it is of faith, that it might be by grace; to the end the promise might be sure to all the seed;

That is, to all believers, who are the true seed of Abraham. He is the father of the faithful, and if thou art one of the faithful, he is thy father; and the covenant which God made with Abraham and his seed was made with thee, and on thy account, if thou art indeed a believer in the Lord Jesus Christ.

Romans 4:16-22. Not to that only which is of the law, but to that also which is of the faith of Abraham; who is the father of us all, (as it is written. I have made thee a father of many nations, before him whom he believed, even God, who quickeneth the dead, and calleth those things which be not as though they were. Who against hope believed in hope, that he might become the father of many nations, according to that which was spoken, So shall thy seed be. And being not weak in faith, he considered not his own body now dead, when he was about an hundred years old, neither yet the deadness of Sarah's womb: He staggered not at the promise of God through unbelief; but was strong in faith, giving glory to God; and being fully persuaded that, what he had promised, he was able also to perform. And therefore it was imputed to him for righteousness..

O soul, if thou art like one who is dead, if thou art devoid of all strength, and grace, and savor, if thou canst but believe in God who can quicken the dead, if thou wilt but trust thy soul in the hands of him who is able even to raise dry bones out of their graves, and make them live, thy faith shall be imputed unto thee for righteousness! Thy faith is that which shall justify thee in the sight of God, and thou shalt be "accepted in the Beloved." Oh, what marvels faith works! This is the root-grace, all manner of good things spring from faith, but there must be faith as the root if there are to be other graces as the fruit. Do thy God the honour to believe him,-to believe that he cannot lie,-to believe that he has never promised what he is not able to perform. If thou wilt do that, it is clear that thou art one of Abraham's seed, and the covenant made with Abraham was made with thee also.

Romans 4:23-25. Now it was not written for his sake alone, that it was imputed to him; but for us also, to whom it shall be imputed, if we believe on him that raised up Jesus our Lord from the dead; who was delivered for our offences, and was raised again for our justification.

See the great object of saving faith,-Christ, once dead, has been raised from the dead, and if thou wouldst be saved, thou must rely upon the crucified and risen Saviour. If thou thus believest that Jesus the crucified is the Christ of God, the anointed Messiah and Redeemer, thou provest that thou art born of God; and if thou trustest thyself to the risen and glorified Christ, thou hast risen in him, and thou shalt rise to be with him for ever and ever.

This exposition consisted of readings from Romans 4, and Romans 5:1-2.

Verses 16-25

Romans 4:16. Therefore it is of faith, that it might be by grace; to the end the promise might be sure to all the seed, not to that only which is of the law, but to that also which is of the faith of Abraham; who is the father of us all,

Abraham is the father of all who believe, whether they be circumcised or not; and the promises made to him belong to them also.

Romans 4:17-18. (As it is written, I have made thee a father of many nations,) before him whom he believed, even God, who quickeneth the dead, and calleth those things which be not as though they were. Who against hope believed in hope, that he might become the father of many nations, according to that which was spoken, So shall thy seed be.

He was an old man, with a very aged wife, yet the Lord promised that he should be "the father of many nations." He firmly believed that which was spoken, and in due time it came to pass.

Romans 4:19-21. And being not weak in faith, he considered not his own body now dead, when he was about an hundred years old, neither yet the deadness of Sarah's womb: he staggered not at the promise of God through unbelief, but was strong in faith, giving glory to God; and being fully persuaded that, what he had promised, he was able also to perform.

That is the kind of faith we want, the faith that does not enquire how God can perform his promise, but believes that he will do it.

Romans 4:22-23. And therefore it was imputed to him for righteousness. Now it was not written for his sake alone, that it was imputed to him

The imputation would be enough for Abraham without any writing; but as it is written, it is for our instruction, and for our comfort.

Romans 4:24-25. But for us also, to whom it shall be imputed, if we believe on him that raised up Jesus our Lord from the dead; who was delivered for our offences, and was raised again for our justification.

May the Lord bless to us our meditation upon this precious portion of his Word!

This exposition consisted of readings from Romans 3, and Romans 4:16-25.

ROMANS 5

Verse 1-2

Romans 5:1. Therefore being justified by faith, we have peace with God through our Lord Jesus Christ:

My friend, are these words true concerning you? Can you put your finger on this verse, and say, "this is true of me, 'Therefore being justified by faith, we have-I have-peace with God through our Lord Jesus Christ'"? We who have believed in Jesus enjoy that peace, a deep, profound calm is upon our spirit whenever we think of God. We are not afraid of him; we are not afraid to meet him even on his judgment-seat: "Being justified by faith, we have peace with God." Have you peace with God? Are you sure that you have it? If not, mayhap you are not justified by faith, for that is the root of it: "Being justified by faith, we have peace with God through our Lord Jesus Christ."

Romans 5:2. By whom also we have access by faith into this grace wherein we stand, and rejoice in hope of the glory of God.

This is a golden staircase, justification brings peace, and peace brings access into this grace wherein we are established; and then comes the joy of hope, and that hope fixes its eye on nothing less than the glory of God. Grace is the stepping-stone to glory; and they who are justified by faith shall in due time be glorified by love.

This exposition consisted of readings from Romans 4, and Romans 5:1-2.

Verses 1-5

Romans 5:1. Therefore-

The apostle Paul had the logical faculty largely developed, so his writings are full of "therefores." And the Christian religion, as a whole, stands logically connected,—doctrine with doctrine, truth with truth. Error is inconsistent with itself, but truth is consistent, logical, and unerring. "Therefore"—

Romans 5:1. Being justified by faith, we have peace with God through our Lord Jesus Christ:

Are you enjoying that peace, dear friend, at this moment? if you are, indeed, justified by faith, you are at peace with God. Therefore, know it, and feel no disquietude. Draw near to God as a dear child might to a loving father. "We have peace with God through our Lord Jesus Christ:—

Romans 5:2. By whom also we have access by faith into this grace wherein we stand, and rejoice in hope of the glory of God.

When a man is at peace with God, then he has the desire to draw near to him. When he is justified, he has the right to draw near; so that, being justified, and having peace, we have access by faith; and this is not a transient privilege, but the grace into which we have access is a grace in which we stand. We abide in it; the Lord has given us, through our justification, a permanent standing near to himself. "We have access by faith into this grace wherein we stand; and this gives us joy,—the joy of sweet hope concerning the bright future that lies before us: "We rejoice in hope of the glory of God."

Romans 5:3. And not only so,—

Whenever the apostle begins to talk of the Lord's bounties to his people, he abounds in "also's" and in "not only so's? As if he had not said enough already, when he had reminded us of the joy of hope in God's glory, he says, "And not only so." We have something in possession as well as something to hope for; we have a present glory as well as glory laid up in store: "And not only so,"—

Romans 5:3-5. But we glory in tribulations also: knowing that tribulation worketh patience; and patience, experience; and experience, hope: and hope maketh not ashamed; because the love of God is shed abroad in our hearts by the Holy Ghost which is given unto us.

Beloved, it is a mark of great grace to be able to acquiesce in tribulation, and to accept it with patient resignation at the Lord's hands; but it is a sign of a still higher state of grace when we glory in tribulation,—when we welcome it and say, "Now, the Lord is about to elevate me to the upper class in his school,—to teach me some deeper truths than I have hitherto learned, to give me a closer acquaintance with some mystery of his kingdom than I have previously had,—to work in my heart some new grace which has never been there before. "We glory in tribulations also: knowing that tribulation worketh patience." You cannot learn to swim on dry land, and you cannot learn to be patient without having something to endure. "Tribulation worketh patience; and patience, experience." There are some who think that they will get; experience through tribulation. So they do, in a certain sense; but not experience of the right kind. There is a middle term—patience,—which keeps its right place: "Tribulation worketh patience; and patience, experience." I know some people, who have had a thousand troubles, but they have no more experience now than they had when they began; I mean, they are just as foolish,—just as untaught in the things of God,—just as ready as before to blunder into a fresh trouble, because they have lacked that middle term. Then, further Paul says, "and experience, hope." Our experience of the Lord's goodness in the past leads us on to hope for still greater things in the future and, thus, experience worketh hope. I have seen some persons, who were called experienced Christians, in whom it seemed to me that experience had worked despair; for their faces were always very long and very sad, and their speech was as dolorous as it well could be. But here I find that true Christian experience worketh hope,—a hope that maketh not ashamed; because the love of God is shed abroad in our hearts by the Holy Ghost which is given unto us."

Verses 1-9

Romans 5:1. Therefore being justified by faith, we have peace with God through our Lord Jesus Christ:

We have it tonight. We enjoy it. We delight in it, "through our Lord Jesus Christ."

Romans 5:2. By whom also we have access by faith into this grace wherein we stand, and rejoice in hope of the glory of God.

Not only have we peace, but we get into the favor of God, and we stand in it. This is the grace or favor which comes of being justified. We feel a freedom now to come into our Father's presence, because he has forgiven us for Christ's sake. We feel at home with him now though once we were prodigal sons, and had wandered far away, and we rejoice in hope of the glory of God. We have something yet in reserve — present peace, but future perfection. We have present rest, but there still remaineth a rest for the people of God. We rejoice in hope of the glory of God.

Romans 5:3-5. And not only so, but we glory in tribulations also: knowing that tribulation worketh patience; And patience, experience; and experience, hope: And hope maketh not ashamed; because the love of God is shed abroad in our hearts by the Holy Ghost which is given unto us.

So that even what might seem to be the disadvantages of this present life are made to work into advantages; and what at one time might threaten our prosperity, really conduces to it. Patience, which we never could have if we never had a trouble, is given to us, and experience, which we never could have if we did not patiently endure the trouble, we obtain. We get pearls out of these deep seas. We get treasures out of these blazing furnaces which seem to smelt our blessings, that they may come to us rich and pure. And, above all, there rises a glorious hope, never to be drowned — never to be made ashamed — because we feel the love of God shed abroad in our hearts like a sweet perfume, making every part of our nature fragrant, because the Holy Ghost is there.

Romans 5:6. For when we were yet without strength, in due time Christ died for the ungodly.

That was our character. There was no good point about us. We were ungodly and we had no strength to mend ourselves or to be other than ungodly. The strength for reformation had all gone. The strength for regeneration we never had. We were without strength, and then Christ died for us — died for the ungodly.

Romans 5:7. For scarcely for a righteous man will one die: yet peradventure for a good man

A benevolent, loving-spirited man.

Romans 5:7-8. Some would even dare to die. But God commendeth his love toward us in that, while we were yet sinners, Christ died for us.

And that is the glory of his love. While we were rebels against his government, he redeemed us. While we were far off from him by wicked works he sent his Son to die and bring us near. Free grace, indeed, was this — not caused by anything in us, but springing freely from the great heart of God.

Romans 5:9. Much more then, being now justified by his blood, we shall be saved from wrath through him.

You see the force of the argument. If he loved us when we were still dead in sin, much more will he keep us and preserve us now that he hath justified us. Were his enemies redeemed? Shall not his friends be kept? Did he love those who were still far off? Will be not love those who are brought near, and love us even to the end?

Verses 1-10

Romans 5:1-3. Therefore being justified by faith, we have peace with God through our Lord Jesus Christ: by whom also we have access by faith into this grace wherein we stand, and rejoice in hope of the glory of God. And not only so, but we glory in tribulations also:

Faith has such wondrous power that it makes us rejoice even in trial; it helps Christians to be glad even in the midst of sorrow.

Romans 5:3. Knowing that tribulation worketh patience; —

The more trial you have the more spiritual education you receive. You cannot learn the virtue of patience without tribulation, any more than a man can learn to be a sailor if he stops on shore: "Tribulation worketh patience;" —

Romans 5:4. And patience, experience;

If you bear the trial patiently, it leaves the mark of its graving tool upon your spirit, and you thus become fashioned into an experienced Christian.

Romans 5:4. And experience, hope:

What God has once done, he may do again; and as he has shown us so much favor we may reasonably hope that he will show us more, and that he who has given us grace will give us glory.

Romans 5:5. And hope maketh not ashamed; —

Our hope brings us courage, no longer are we trembling and diffident, but we feel like children do towards a loving father, we are happily, restfully at home with our God. " Hope maketh not ashamed; " —

Romans 5:5. Because the love of God is shed abroad in our hearts by the Holy Ghost which is given unto us.

When Mary, the sister of Lazarus, anointed the feet of Jesus with the very costly ointment of spikenard, "the house was filled with the odour" of it, and in a similar fashion the love of God perfumes every part of our nature.

Romans 5:6. For when we were yet without strength, in due time Christ died for the ungodly."

What a wonderful statement! "Christ died for the ungodly." Yet it was no slip of the pen, for the apostle takes up his own expression, and preaches the following little sermon upon it: —

Romans 5:7. For scarcely for a righteous man will one die:

If a man is known to be sternly just, like Aristides, nobody would care enough for him to die for him.

Romans 5:7. Yet peradventure for a good man some would even dare to die.

For a benevolent man, a true philanthropist, a lover of his race, there are some who might say that they would die for him. Yet the apostle only says, "Peradventure for a good man some would even dare to die." It is not very likely, but it is just possible.

Romans 5:8. But God commendeth his love toward us, in that, while we were yet sinners, Christ died for us.

Certainly we were not "good" men, we were not even "just" men, but we are included in this black description "sinners"; and "while we were yet sinners, Christ died for us." He died for us as sinners, he did not come to save saints, but to save sinners; and it was for sinners that he died.

Romans 5:9. Much more than, being now justified by his blood, we shall be saved from wrath through him.

This is a fine piece of argument, and strictly logical. If, when we were sinners, Christ died for us, will he let us be condemned now that he has washed us in his precious blood? Is it possible that, after dying for us, he will let us fall from grace, and perish after all? That will never be. Notice the same kind of argument again: —

Romans 5:10. For if, when we were enemies, we were reconciled to God by the death of his Son, much more, being reconciled, we shall be saved by his life.

There is a threefold argument here. If Christ died for us when we were his enemies, will he not save us now that we are his friends? If he died to reconcile us to God, will he not completely save us now that this great work has been accomplished? And as we were reconciled to God by Christ's death, shall we not much more be saved by his life? There are three arguments, and each one is sound and conclusive. The believer in Jesus must be eternally saved. If Christ died for sinners, what will he not do for believers, who are no longer enemies, but are reconciled unto God by the death of his Son?

This exposition consisted of readings from Romans 5:1-10; and 2 Corinthians 4; and 2 Corinthians 5.

Verses 1-11

Romans 5:1. Therefore being justified by faith, —

But why "therefore"? Because of the verge preceding it: "Who was delivered for our offences, and was raised again for our justification." Christ died to atone for our sins, Christ rose again to secure our justification, "Therefore being justified by faith," —

Romans 5:1. We have peace with God through our lord Jesus Christ;

We have peace, we know that we have, we enjoy it, it is not a thing of the future, we have peace, a deep calm like that which came to the disciples when Christ hushed the winds and waves to sleep. "We have peace with God," his peace has entered into us, we possess it now; but it is all "through our Lord Jesus Christ." It is all war apart from him, but all peace through him. We poor sinners, being justified by faith, have peace with God through our Lord Jesus Christ.

Romans 5:2. By whom also we have access by faith —

That is to say, we come near to God; we have the entry of the King's palace; "we have access by faith" —

Romans 5:2. Into this grace wherein we stand,

With firm foot and confident heart, we stand in God's presence. Happy people!

Romans 5:2. And rejoice in hope of the glory of God.

What a window hope is! It looks toward heaven; we have only to look out that way, and then we can "rejoice in hope of the glory of God."

Romans 5:3. And not only so, but we glory —

We hope for glory, — "the glory of God," and we already "glory." But in what do we glory? " We glory" —

Romans 5:3. In tribulations also: —

That is the blackest thing a Christian has, — his tribulations; so, if we can glory in them, surely we can glory in anything. "We glory in tribulations also:" —

Romans 5:3. Knowing that tribulation worketh patience;

A man cannot prove that he has patience if he has never been tried. Christian patience is not a weed, it is a cultivated plant; we only get patience through our trials.

Romans 5:4. And patience, experience; and experience, hope:

You cannot make an experienced Christian without trouble. You cannot make an old sailor on shore, nor make a good soldier without fighting. Here is that window of hope again, standing at the back of our experience, we look out of the window, and what God has done for us is a token of what God will do for us.

Romans 5:5. And hope maketh not ashamed;

Peace gives us courage, hope takes the blush out of the cheek when we confess Christ, for we remember the glory that is to be revealed in him and in us, so how can shame come in?

Romans 5:5. Because the love of God is shed abroad in our hearts by the Holy Ghost which is given unto us.

God's love is like sweet perfume in an alabaster box; the Holy Spirit breaks that box, pours out the love of God into our souls, and the perfume fills our entire nature.

Romans 5:6. For when we were yet without strength, in due time Christ died for the ungodly."

When we had no power to do anything that was good, when we were strengthless and hopeless, then Christ died for us. This is a wonderful gospel expression, which ought to bring comfort to those here who have no pretence of godliness, "Christ died for the ungodly."

Romans 5:7. For scarcely for a righteous man will one die:

However upright and just a man may be, nobody thinks of dying for him.

Romans 5:7. Yet peradventure for a good man some would even dare to die.

That is to say, for a generous, kind, noble-hearted man, some might dare to die.

Romans 5:8. But God commendeth his love toward us, in that, while we were yet sinners, Christ died for us.

We were neither righteous nor yet good, yet Christ died for us. "Oh!" said a little boy once to his mother, "I do not think so much of Christ dying for men, I think I would be willing to die if I could save a hundred men by dying." But his mother said," Suppose it was a hundred mosquitoes, — would you die for them?" "Oh, no!" he said, "I would let the whole lot of them die." Well, we were much less, in comparison with Christ than mosquitoes are in relation to men, yet he died for us, good-for-nothing creatures that we are. Well does one say, "God shows part of his love to us in many different ways, but he shows the whole of his love in giving Christ to die for us." Here you see his heart laid bare, the very heart of God laid open for the inspection of every believing soul. To die for saints would be great love; but to die for sinners, while they are yet sinners, and regarding them as sinners, — this is love with emphasis, the very highest commendation that even divine love can have.

Romans 5:9. Much more then, being now justified by his blood, we shall be saved from wrath through him.

See; it is a less thing for God to preserve us when we are justified than it is for him to justify us while we are yet sinners. The final perseverance of the saints may well be argued from their conversion, their entrance into glory is guaranteed by the ransom price that Christ has paid for their redemption. He died to save sinners, so how is it possible that he should let saints perish? Oh, no; that can never be! "Much more then, being now justified by his blood, we shall be saved from wrath through him."

Romans 5:10. For if, when we were enemies, we were reconciled to God by the death of his Son, much more, being reconciled, we shall be saved by his life.

Notice that while we were his enemies, he blessed us, so now that we are reconciled to him, will he not still bless us? If he reconciled us to him by the death of his son, will he not save us by his life now that we are reconciled to him? Does he make us his friends, intending afterwards to destroy us? Perish such a thought. This verge is like a trident, it is a three-pronged argument for our eternal safety. I will read it again: "For if, when we were enemies, we were reconciled to God by the death of his Son, much more, being reconciled, we shall be raved by his life."

Romans 5:11. And not only so, —

Surely we have got high enough when we have reached an absolute certainty of our eternal salvation. Yet we are to go still higher: "And not only so," —

Romans 5:11. But we also joy in God —

Even now we joy in God, "although the fig tree shall not blossom, neither shall fruit be in the vines; the labour of the olives shall fail, and the field shall yield no meat; the flock shall be cut off from the fold, and there shall be no herd in the stalls," yet do "we joy in God" —

Romans 5:11. Through our Lord Jesus Christ, —

Every blessing comes to us through him. How Paul delights to harp upon that string! He says continually, "through our Lord Jesus Christ," —

Romans 5:11. By whom we have now received the atonement.

Through our Lord Jesus Christ, we are at one with God, we are reconciled to him by the death of his Son. All our sin is for ever put away we have received the atonement, and we rejoice in the God of our salvation Glory be to his holy name for ever and ever!

Verses 1-21

Romans 5:1. Therefore being justified by faith, we have peace with God through our Lord Jesus Christ:

These are matters of fact; not of fanatical delusion, but of logical conclusion, for Paul begins with a "therefore." God's people are justified on solid grounds, on reasonable grounds, on grounds that will bear the test even of the last great judgment day. "therefore, being " — now, at the present time, this very moment, — " justified by faith, we have peace:" not only we hope to have it, and trust we shall have it, but we have it. "We have peace," — not only peace of conscience, and peace with our fellow-men, but "we have peace with God through our Lord Jesus Christ.:' Mark that; we have it. O dear people of God, do not be satisfied unless you can talk in this confident fashion: "therefore being justified by faith, we have peace with God through our Lord Jesus Christ."

Romans 5:2. By whom also —

What! is not that first verse all? Oh, no! there is more to follow. When you get a hold of one golden link of the blessed chain of grace, it pulls up another, and then another, and then another: "By whom also " —

Romans 5:2. We have access by faith into this grace wherein we stand,

We come into this grace by Jesus Christ, and to this heavenly standing, this justified condition, through Jesus Christ who is the door.

Romans 5:2. And rejoice in hope of the glory ofGod.

Our joy is in the past and the present in some measure, but it is still more in the future: "We rejoice in hope of the glory of God." We have three windows. — the one out of which we look back with gratitude upon the past, the one out of which we look with joy in the present, and the one out of which we look with expectation upon the future.

Romans 5:3. And not only so,-

There is for every child of God grace upon grace; every line of the apostle's writing tells of more blessing: "And not only so." Is not that enough? Justified, enjoying peace, having access into grace, rejoicing in hope of the glory of God; what can there be more? Why, there is something on the road as well as at the end of it: "And not only so,"-

Romans 5:3. But we glory in tribulations also: —

We are not only acquiescent in the divine will; but, tutored by the Spirit of God, we come even to "glory in tribulations also: " —

Romans 5:3. Knowing that tribulation worketh patience; —

"Knowing." Paul was no agnostic, he was a "knowing" man, and all God's people ought to be the same. they are a very dogmatic people when they are what they ought to be; they have nothing to do with "ifs ", and "ands", and "butt", and "peradventures"; but they believe and are sure: "Knowing that tribulation worketh patience." the natural tendency of tribulation is to work impatience, it produces peevishness in many; but where the Spirit of God is, there is a heavenly counteraction of natural tendencies, and "tribulation worketh patience;" —

Romans 5:4. And patience, experience; and experience, hope:

Again I cannot help observing how we seem to go through one door just to pass through another. We get into a silver chamber that we may go into a golden one; and before we can take stock of all the gold, we are ushered into a gorgeous palace of pearls and rubies and diamonds of priceless value.

Romans 5:5. And hope maketh not ashamed; because the love of God is shed abroad in our hearts by the Holy Ghost which is given unto us.

If you have the Holy Ghost given unto you, then the love of God fills your nature like a sweet perfume. As when the woman broke the alabaster box, and the house was filled with the odor of the ointment, so, when the Spirit of God comes, and brings the broken alabaster of the Saviour's sacrifice, and we feel the love of God poured out among us, what a delightful perfume there is! "thy name is as ointment poured forth, therefore do the virgins love thee." the way to make us love God is for the love of God to be shed abroad in our hearts by the Holy Ghost.

Romans 5:6. for when we were yet without strength, in due time Christ died for the ungodly.

Are not these very wonderful words? "Christ died for the ungodly." Pick out all those who are the naturally good people, and this text has nothing to do with them; but find out the ungodly, the sinful, the wicked, and here is a text exactly suitable for them: "Christ died for the ungodly."

Romans 5:7. for scarcely for a righteous man will one die:

He is very righteous, but he is very stern; nobody cares much about him.

Romans 5:7. Yet peradventure for a good man some would even dare to die.

He is "a good man " — benevolent, kind, and tender.

Romans 5:8. But God commendeth his love toward us, in that, while we were yet sinners, Christ died for us.

While we were neither righteous nor good, "while we were yet sinners, Christ" did the most he ever could, or ever can do for us, he "died for us." this is the best gift for the worst of men, and that best gift given to them when they are at their worst state: "While we were yet sinners, Christ died for us."

Romans 5:9. Much more then, being now justified by his blood, we shall be saved from wrath through him.

"Much more." Paul has been giving us "alsos" and "ands"; now he takes a bigger leap still, for he says, "Much more then, being now justified by his blood, we shall be saved from wrath through him." If he saved us when we were sinners, he will certainly save us now that we are justified. If he called us when we were dead, he will not leave us now we are alive.

Romans 5:10. For if, when we were enemies, we were reconciled to God by the death of his Son, much more, being reconciled, we shall be saved by his life.

You see, there are three points here. When we were enemies, he blessed us; much more, now that we are reconciled, will he do so. If, in the second place, when we were enemies he reconciled us, how much more, after he has reconciled us, will he save us! And, thirdly, if he did all this for us by the death of his Son, much more will he do for us by his life; reconciled by his death, we shall be saved by his life.

Romans 5:11. And not only so,-

there is no end to the blessing, dear brethren and sisters. the apostle seems to be always going up, and up, and up. this Paul, calm and cool and logical as he is, makes the fire burn most wondrously: "And not only so," —

Romans 5:11. But we also joy in God —

We are glad that he is God, glad that he is such a God as he is; we would not wish to have him altered. the God of Abraham, and of Isaac, and of Jacob, — the God of the Old testament, and the God of the New testament, — we love him altogether just as he is, and "we joy in God —

Romans 5:11-21. through our Lord Jesus Christ, by whom we have now received the atonement. Wherefore, as by one man sin entered into the world, and death by sin; and so death passed upon all men, for that all have sinned .. (for until the law sin was in the world: but sin is not imputed when there is no law. Nevertheless death reigned from Adam to Moses, even over them that had not sinned after the similitude of Adam's transgression, who is the figure of him that was to come. But not as the offence, so also is the free gift. For if through the offence of one many be dead, much more the grace of God, and the gift by grace, which is by one man, Jesus Christ, hath abounded unto many. And not as it was by one that sinned, so is the gift: for the judgment was by one to condemnation, but the free gift is of many offences unto justification. for if by one man's offence death reigned by one; much more they which receive abundance of grace and of the gift of righteousness shall reign in life by one, Jesus Christ.) Therefore as by the offence of one judgment came upon all men to condemnation; even so by the righteousness of one the free gift came upon all men unto justification of life. For as by one man's disobedience many were made sinners, so by the obedience of one shall many be made righteous. Moreover the law entered, that the offence might abound. But where sin abounded, grace did much more abound: that as sin hath reigned unto death, even so might grace reign through righteousness unto eternal life by Jesus Christ our Lord.

I have not expounded the latter part of the chapter, as time fades me, and I shall dwell upon it somewhat in the sermon.

This exposition consisted of readings from Jonah 3; Jonah 4:1-2; and Romans 5.

Verses 6-11

Romans 5:6. For then we were yet without strength, in due time Christ died for the ungodly.

What a wonderful sentence that is! Not, "Christ died for the saints, "not, "Christ died for righteous men;" but, "when we were yet without strength, in due time Christ died for the ungodly."

Romans 5:7-9. For scarcely for a righteous man will one die: yet peradventure for a good man some would even dare to die. But God commendeth his love toward us, in that, while we were yet sinners, Christ died for us. Much more then, being now justified by his blood, we shall be saved from wrath through him.

What an argument this is for the final safety of believers! If Christ died for us when we were enemies, surely he will give us now that he has died for us and made us his friends, his reconciled subject": "Much more then, being now justified by his blood, we shall be saved from wrath through him."

Romans 5:10. For if, when we were enemies, we were reconciled to God by the death of his Son, much more, being reconciled, we shall be saved by his life.

There is a threefold argument there. We were enemies, yet God blessed us even then, so will he not bless us even more now that we are reconciled to him? When we were enemies, he reconciled us unto himself. Having done that, will he not certainly save us? We were reconciled to God by the death of his Son; so much more shall we be saved by the life of the risen and glorified Jesus, which has almighty, irresistible power.

Romans 5:11. And not only so, but we also joy in God through our Lord Jesus Christ, by whom we have now received the atonement.

This exposition consisted of readings from Romans 3:9-27; Romans 5:6-11; Romans 8:1-32.

Verses 6-21

Romans 5:6. For when we were yet without strength, in due time Christ died for the ungodly.

This is one of the most surprising sentences on record. If it had not been inspired, there are many who would cavil at it. Indeed, many do cavil at it even now, for it is still currently believed that Christ must have died for the righteous. Yet thus is it written: "In due time Christ died for the ungodly." And this is the commendation of that death, and of the love which suggested it:—

Romans 5:7. For scarcely for a righteous man will one die:

For a merely just man, scarcely would anybody die.

Romans 5:7. Yet peradventure for a good man—

For a benevolent man—

Romans 5:7-8. Some would even dare to die. But God commendeth his love toward us, in that, while we were yet sinners, Christ died for us,

It is under that aspect that Christ is to be regarded as dying for the ungodly, dying for sinners. Ungodly man, guilty sinner, is there not hope for you in this blessed truth? Does anyone say, "I shall be lost, for I am ungodly; I must necessarily perish, for I am a sinner"? Your logic is at fault, dear friend. "Christ died for the ungodly;" "while we were yet sinners, Christ died for us;" therefore, the ungodly,—sinners—be saved because of his death, and all who trust him shall be saved.

Romans 5:9. Much more then, being now justified by his blood, we shall be saved from wrath through him.

Did he die for us while we were sinners? Will he not, then, surely keep us now that we are Saved? Yes, that he will.

66

Romans 5:10. For if, when we were enemies, we were reconciled to God by the death of his Son, much more, being reconciled, we shall be saved by his life.

What an invincible argument this is for the safety of all true believers in Jesus! Did he die for them, and reconcile them unto his Father by his death, when they were enemies? Then, will he not certainly save them now that they are reconciled, seeing that he ever lives to intercede for them? Will he not save them by his life? Assuredly, he will.

Romans 5:11. And not only so,—

We cannot get to the end of these priceless boons. These precious pearls are too numerous even for the apostle to count, although he was a man who knew how to "reckon" up spiritual treasures: "And not only so,"—

Romans 5:11-14. But we also joy in God through our Lord Jesus Christ, by whom we have now received the atonement. Wherefore, as by one man sin entered into the world, and death by sin; and so death passed upon all men, for that all have sinned: (For until the law sin was in the world: but sin is not imputed when there is no law. Nevertheless death reigned from Adam to Moses, even over them that had not sinned—

Personally—

Romans 5:14. After the similitude of Adam's transgression, who is the figure of him that was to come.

So that the sin of Adam took effect upon the human race before the law came, and even Upon those who had no personal transgression,— unconscious infants, I mean,—causing them to die.

Romans 5:15-17. But not as the offence, so also is the free gift. For if through the offence of one many be dead, much more the grace of God, and the gift by grace, which is by one man, Jesus Christ, hath abounded unto many. And not as it was by one that sinned, so is the gift: for the judgment was by one to condemnation, but the free gift is of many offences unto justification. For if by one man's offence –

By Adam's one sin,—the sin of one man,—

Romans 5:17-18. Death reigned by one; much more they which receive abundance of grace and of the gift of righteousness shall reign in life by one, Jesus Christ.) Therefore as by the offence of one judgment came upon all men to condemnation; even so by the righteousness of one the free gift came upon all men unto justification of life.

That is to say, upon the "all" who are in Christ, as the condemnation came upon the "all" who were in the first Adam. He who believeth not in Jesus has no part in "the free gift unto justification of life;" but he who believeth is a partaker of the glorious justification which comes by Christ.

Romans 5:19-20. For as by one man's disobedience many were made sinners, so by the obedience of one shall many be made righteous. Moreover the law entered, that the offence might abound."

It was the practical result of the giving of the law that men became greater sinners than they were before, and it was the design of the law that they should see themselves to be greater sinners than before. The law is the looking-glass in which we see our spots, but it is not the basin in which we wash them away. The law has a provoking power, for such is-the perversity of our nature that, no sooner do we hear the command, "You shall not do so-and-so," than at once we want to do it. Our nature is very much like quicklime. Throw cold water upon it, and straightway it generateth heat; acting, as it were, against the nature of that which is cast upon it. So, the more God says to a man, "Thou shalt," the more the man says, "I will not;" and the more God says to him, "Thou shalt not," the more doth the man resolve that he will. "The law entered, that the offence might abound." It reveals the depravity and disobedience of human nature, and lays us low before God as convicted criminals.

Romans 5:20. But where sin abounded, grace did much more abound:

Blessed be God for that! Sin may be a river, but grace is an ocean. Sin may be a mountain, but grace is like Noah's flood, which prevailed over the tops of the mountains fifteen cubits upward.

Romans 5:21. That as sin hath reigned unto death, even so might grace reign through righteousness unto eternal life by Jesus Christ our Lord.

Do you know, dear friends, by personal experience, all about this of which we have been reading? I know that many of you do. Would God that all did,—that they understood, by a living faith, what it is to be justified, having first understood, by sorrowful experience, what a sense of condemnation the guilty soul must feel. The Lord bring you all to himself, by Jesus Christ! Amen.

Verses 10-21

Romans 5:10. For if, when we were enemies, we were reconciled to God, by the death of his Son, much more, being reconciled, we shall by saved by his life.

Grand argument for the safety of all believers having a three-fold edge to it. If he reconciled his enemies, will he not save his friends? If he reconciled us, will he not save us? If he reconciled us by the death, will he not save us by the life of his Son?

Romans 5:11. And not only so,

The blessings of the covenant of grace rise tier upon tier, mountain upon mountain, Alp on Alp. When you climb to what seems the utmost summit, there is a height yet beyond you. "And not only so" —

Romans 5:11. But we also joy in God through our Lord Jesus Christ, by whom we have now received the atonement.

Then he begins to explain the great plan of our salvation.

Romans 5:12. Wherefore as by one man sin entered into the world, and death by sin; and so death passed upon all men, for that all have sinned:

In that one man.

Romans 5:13-14. For until the law sin was in the world: but sin is not imputed when there is no law. Nevertheless death reigned from Adam to Moses, even over them that had not sinned after the similitude of Adam's transgression, who is the figure of him that was to come.

Children died who had not actually sinned themselves, but died because of Adam's sin.

Romans 5:15-17. But not as the offence, so also is the free gift. For if through the offence of one many be dead, much more the grace of God, and the gift by grace, which is by one man, Jesus Christ, hath abounded unto many. And not as it was by one that sinned, so is the gift: for the judgment was by one to condemnation, but the free gift is of many offences unto justification. For if by one man's offence—

By Adams' sin.

Romans 5:17-18. Death reigned by one: much more they which receive abundance of grace and of the gift of righteousness shall reign in life by one, Jesus Christ. Therefore, as by the offence of one judgment cam upon all men to condemnation: even so by the righteousness of one the free gift came upon all men unto justification of life.

All who are in Christ are justified by Christ, just as all who were in Adam were lost and condemned in Adam. The "alls" are not equal in extent — equal as far as the person goes in whom the "alls" were found. And this is our hope — that we, being in Christ are justified because of his righteousness.

Romans 5:19-20. For as by one man's disobedience many were made sinners, so by the obedience of one shall many be made righteous. Moreover the law entered,

The law of Moses.

Romans 5:20. That the offence might abound, but where sin abounded, grace did much more abound:

It makes us see sin where we never saw it. It comes on purpose to drive us to despair of being saved by works. It bids us look to the flames that Moses saw, and shrink and tremble with despair.

Romans 5:21. That as sin hath reigned unto death, even so might grace reign through righteousness unto eternal life by Jesus Christ our Lord.

This exposition consisted of readings from Psalms 116:1-6; Romans 5:10-21.

ROMANS 6

Verses 1-19

Paul finishes the last chapter by saying, "That as sin hath reigned unto death, even so might grace reign through righteousness unto eternal life by Jesus Christ our Lord." "What shall we say, then?" What inference shall we draw from the super-abounding of grace over sin?

Romans 6:1. What shall we say then? Shall we continue in sin, that grace may abound?

"Shall we continue in sin, that grace may abound?" That were very horrible inference. It is one great instance of the shocking depravity of man that the inference has been drawn sometimes, I hope not often, for surely Satan himself might scarcely draw an inference of licentiousness from love. Still, some have drawn it.

Romans 6:2. God forbid. How shall we, that are dead to sin, live any longer therein?

Now, he goes on by an argument to prove that those in whom the grace of God has wrought the wondrous change cannot possibly choose sin, nor live in it.

Romans 6:3. Know ye not, that so many of us as were baptized into Jesus Christ were baptized into his death?

That is the very hinge of our religion. His death, not into his example merely, nor primarily into his life, but "into his death." In this we have believed — with a dying Saviour we are linked, and our baptism sets this forth. We "were baptized into his death."

Romans 6:4. Therefore we are buried with him by baptism into death: that like as Christ was raised up from the dead by the glory of the Father, even so we also should walk in the newness of life.

The operations, therefore, of the Spirit of God forbid that a saved man should live in sin. He is dead; he is raised into newness of life: at the very entrance into the church, in the very act of baptism, he declares that he cannot live as he once did, for he is dead: he declares that he must live after another fashion, for has not he been raised again in the type and raised again in very deed from the dead?

Romans 6:5-6. For if we have been planted together in the likeness of his death, we shall be also in the likeness of his resurrection: Knowing this, that our old man is crucified with him, that the body of sin might be destroyed, that henceforth we should not serve sin.

There has a death taken place in us, and though there be relics of corruption still alive, yet they are crucified: they will have to die, they must die they are nailed fast to the cross to die in union with the death of Christ.

Romans 6:7. For he that is dead is freed from sin.

The man is dead. The law cannot ask more of a criminal than to yield his life. If, therefore, he should live again after death, he would not be one who could suffer for his past offences. They were committed in another life, and "he that is dead is freed from sin."

Romans 6:8-9. Now if we be dead with Christ, we believe that we shall also live with him: Knowing that Christ being raised from the dead dieth no more; death hath no more dominion over him.

Or, death will have dominion over him no more: he will never come a second time under death, and neither shall his people. "For in that he died, he died unto sin once." There was an end of it in the sense of once for all, no second death for Christ.

Romans 6:10-12. For in that he died, he died unto sin once: but in that he liveth unto God. Likewise reckon ye also yourselves to be dead indeed unto sin, but alive unto God through Jesus Christ our Lord. Let not sin therefore reign in your mortal body, that ye should obey it in the lusts thereof.

Peradventure, there were some who would say that in their spirits truth and righteousness were supreme, but that in their bodies sin had the mastery Aye, but that will not do. There must be left no lurking piece for sin within the complete system of our manhood: it must be hunted out and hunted down thoroughly, out of the body as well as out of the mind.

Romans 6:13. Neither yield ye your members as instruments of unrighteousness unto sin: but yield yourselves unto God, as those that are alive from the dead and your members as instruments of righteousness unto God.

We do not, I think, make enough of the passive part of our religion We are often for doing, and quite right, too, and the more active we can be the better; still, before the doing there must come a yielding, because we remember who it is that worketh in us, "both to will and to do of his own good pleasure," and our activities after all are not so much our own as we deem, if they are right. They are the activities of the divine life within us, of the Spirit of God himself working in us to the glory of the Father. One great point, therefore, is to yield ourselves up, our members, to be weapons in God's hands for the fighting of the spiritual war.

Romans 6:14. For sin shall not have domination over you: for ye are not under the law, but under grace.

The reigning, ruling principle now, is not "You must, you shall," for reward, or under fear of punishment, but God has loved you, and now you love him in return and what you do springs from no mercenary or self-serving motive. You are not under law, but under grace; yet in another sense you never were so much under law as you are now, for grace puts about you a blessedly sweet, delightful law, which has power over us as the word of command never had. "I will write my law in their hearts, in their inward parts will I write them." Aye, that is the glory of the new life, the delight of him who hath passed from death unto life.

Romans 6:15. What then? shall we sin, because we are not under the law, but under grace?

Oh! this old question keeps coming up. Somebody wants to sin. Well, if he wants to sin, why does not he leave this business alone and go and sin? What has he to do with these theological questions at all? But still, he wants, if he can, to make a coverlet for his wickedness; he wants to enjoy the sweets of the child of God, and yet live like an enemy of God, and so he pops in his head over and over again: "May we not sin because of this or that?" To which the apostle answers again, "God forbid." Oh! may God always forbid it to you, and to me: may the question never be tolerated among us.

Romans 6:15-16. God forbid. Know ye not, that to whom ye yield yourselves servants to obey, his servants ye are to whom ye obey; whether of sin unto death, or of obedience unto righteousness?

If you are doing the deeds of sin, you are the servants of sin and only as you are doing the will of God can you claim to be the servant of God. "Hereby we know that we know him, if we keep his commandments." That becomes the index of our condition. The man, then, that lives in sin and loves it, need not talk about the grace of God he is a stranger to it, for the mark of those that come under grace is this, that they serve God, and no longer serve sin.

Romans 6:17-18. But God be thanked, that ye were the servants of sin, but ye have obeyed from the heart that form of doctrine which was delivered you. Being then made free from sin, ye became the servants of righteousness.

"Bondservants," you have got in our new translation, for so it was, and the apostle seems to excuse himself for using such a word by saying: —

Romans 6:19. I speak after the manner of men because of the infirmity of your flesh: for as ye have yielded your members servants to uncleanness and to iniquity unto iniquity; even so now yield your members servants to righteousness unto holiness.

As you submitted yourselves to sin most cheerfully and voluntarily, and yet were slaves under it, so now come, and be slaves under Christ with most blessed cheerfulness and delight: endeavor now to lose your very wills in his will, for no man's slavery is so complete as his who even yields his will. Now, yield everything to Christ. You shall never be so free as when you do that, never so blessedly delivered from all bondage as when you absolutely and completely yield yourselves up to the power and supremacy of your Lord.

Verses 1-23

Romans 6:1. What shall we say then? Shall we continue in sin, that grace may abound?

The fifth chapter ends up in this way, that "where sin abounded, etc... Jesus Christ our Lord." Then he goes on to say, "What shall we say then?" What inference shall we draw from the fact that where sin abounded, grace did much more abound? Shall we be base enough to draw a wicked inference from a gracious statement? Shall we continue in sin that grace may abound? It is a horrible suggestion, and yet it is one which has come into the minds of many men, for some men are bad enough for anything; they will curdle the sweet milk of love into the sourest argument for sin. "Shall we continue in sin, that grace may abound? God forbid." With all the vehemence of his nature, he saith: —

Romans 6:2. God forbid. How shall we, that are dead to sin, live any longer therein?

The grace of God makes us dead to sin. This is the grace of God, which delivers us from the power of evil, and if this be so, how can we live any longer therein?

Romans 6:3. Know ye not, that so many of us as were baptized into Jesus Christ were baptized into his death?

If we are in Christ at all, we are partakers of his death; and as his was a death for sin and a death to sin, we are made partakers of it; we are really dead because Christ died, and we are in him. Therefore we are dead to the old life, to the old way of sin. We signify that by our baptism.

Romans 6:4. Therefore we are buried with him by baptism into death: that like as Christ was raised up from the dead by the glory of the Father, even so we also should walk in newness of life.

Our baptism, solemn as it was, was a great acted falsehood, a living pretense, unless we are dead to our former way of living, and have come to live unto God in a new life altogether, by virtue of the resurrection of Christ from the dead.

Romans 6:5. For if we have been planted together in the likeness of his death, we shall be also in the likeness of his resurrection:

If we have partaken of his death, we partake also of his rising power. We live because he lives, and we live as he lives, not after the old manner, but in newness of life.

Romans 6:6. Knowing this, that our old man is crucified with him, that the body of sin might be destroyed, that henceforth we should not serve sin.

We are to regard ourselves as persons that have been dead. We are ourselves, it is true; and yet in another sense we are not our own selves. We are not to look upon ourselves as though we owed any kind of service to the power which we obeyed before we knew the Lord. We are new people, we have got a new life, and have entered upon a new existence — the old man is crucified with him

Romans 6:7-8. For he that is dead is freed from sin. Now if we be dead with Christ, we believe that we shall also live with him:

There was no getting free from the power of sin, except by dying to it; but, being dead to it, we are free from it; and, now being dead that way, we have entered into a new life that we might live as Christ lives.

Romans 6:9. Knowing that Christ being raised from the dead dieth no more; death hath no more dominion over him.

So we, being raised from our former death, shall die no more; death hath no more dominion over us. That is to say, sin cannot reign in us again; we are dead to it, we are brought into a new life that can never end, even as our Lord Jesus Christ is. There is a parallel between us and Christ, even as there is a union between us.

Romans 6:10. For in that he died, he died unto sin once: but in that he liveth, he liveth unto God.

And so do we; we have died unto sin once, but now that we live, we live unto God.

Romans 6:11-12. Likewise reckon ye also yourselves to be dead indeed unto sin, but alive unto God through Jesus Christ our Lord. Let not sin therefore reign in your mortal body, that ye should obey it in the lusts thereof.

It is in the body that it tries to reign. These poor things, these mortal frames of ours, have so many passions, so many desires, so many weak-messes, all of which are apt to bring us under the dominion of sin, unless we watch with great care.

Romans 6:13. Neither yield ye your members as instruments of unrighteousness unto sin: but yield yourselves unto God, as those that are alive from the dead, and your members as instruments of righteousness unto God.

"Neither yield ye your members as instruments of unrighteousness unto sin" — neither eyes, nor ears, nor hands, nor feet, neither suffer any of these to become the tools of sin, "but yield yourselves unto God." He is ready to use you, lay all the powers of your nature out as tools, for him to use. "Yield yourselves unto God as those that are alive from the dead." He is not the God of the dead; he cannot use the dead, but he is the God of the living, and as you profess to have received a new life in Christ, yield up all the faculties of this new life unto the living God, "and your members as instruments of righteousness unto God."

Romans 6:14. For sin shall not have dominion over you: for ye are not under the law, but under grace.

When you were under the law, sin did get dominion over you; that law which was ordained to life, worked towards death. The evil concupiscence of your nature revolted against the command, and led you astray. But now, beloved, it is of love and grace, and now sin cannot get in: stronger motives shall hold you to holiness than ever held you before, and the grace of Go itself, like a wall of fire, shall guard you from the dominion of sin.

Romans 6:15. What then? shall we sin because we are not under the law, but under grace? God forbid.

That must not be. Again the evil spirit crops up, trying to turn the grace of God into licentiousness, and to make us feel free to sin because of God's love — that must not be.

Romans 6:16. Know ye not, that to whom ye yield yourselves servants to obey, his servants ye are to whom ye obey; whether of sin unto death, or of obedience unto righteousness?

It is a wonderful heart-searching text, is this: let us put ourselves under its power. Whatever you obey, that is your master: and if you obey the suggestions of sin, you are the slave of sin: and it is only as you are obedient to God that you are truly the servants of God. So that, after all, our outward, walk and conversation are the best test of our true condition. Without holiness no man shall see the Lord, nor can. he have any reason to believe that he belongs to God.

Romans 6:17. But God be thanked, that ye were the servants of sin, but ye have obeyed from the heart that form of doctrine which was delivered you.

Or into which you were delivered. God has taken you, melted you down, and poured you into a new mold. God be thanked for flint; you are not what you used to be. Although you are not what you hope to be, yet you have reason to bless God you are not what once you were-you have obeyed from the heart that form of doctrine into which you were delivered.

Romans 6:18. Being then made free from sin, ye became the servants of righteousness.

The fetters are struck off, the lusts of the flesh do not hold us any longer. We are the Lord's free men, and out of gratitude for this glorious freedom, we become the willing servants of the righteous God.

Romans 6:19. I speak after the manner of men because of the infirmity of your flesh: for as ye have yielded your members servants to uncleanness and to iniquity unto iniquity; even so now yield your members servants to righteousness unto holiness.

It wants no explanation. In the days of our sin, we sinned with all our power. There was not one part of us but what became the willing servant of sin: and we went from iniquity into iniquity, and now the Cross has made us entirely new, and we have been melted down, poured out into a fresh mold. Now, let us yield every member of our body, soul, and spirit to righteousness, even unto holiness, till the whole of us, in the wholeness and consequently the holiness of our nature, shall be given unto God.

Romans 6:20. For when ye were the servants of sin, ye were free from righteousness.

You did not care about righteousness then. When you served sin you felt it was utterly indifferent to you what the claims of righteousness might be. Well, now that you have become the servant of righteousness, be free from sin, let sin have no more dominion over you now, than righteousness used to have when you were the slaves of sin. "What fruit had ye then in those things whereof ye are now ashamed?" What profit did they ever bring you? There was a temporary delight, like the blossom on the tree in spring, but what fruit find you? Did it ever come, to anything? Is there anything to look back upon with pleasure in a life of sin? Oh no, those things whereof we are now ashamed were fruitless to us, "for the end of those things is death."

Romans 6:22-23. But now being made free from sin, and become servants to God, ye have your fruit unto holiness, and the end everlasting life. For the wages of sin is death; but the gift of God is eternal life through Jesus Christ our Lord.

ROMANS 7

Verses 1-25

Romans 7:1-3. Know ye not, brethren, (for I speak to them that know the law,) how that the law hath dominion over a man as long as he liveth? For the woman which hath an husband is bound by the law to her husband so long as he liveth; but if the husband be dead, she is loosed from the law of her husband. So then if, while her husband liveth, she be married to another man, she shall be called an adulteress, but if her husband be dead, she is free from that law; so that she is no adulteress, though she be married to another man.

He merely states this as an illustration.

Romans 7:4. Wherefore, my brethren, ye also are become dead to the law by the body of Christ; that ye should be married to another, even to him who is raised from the dead, that we should bring forth fruit unto God.

While we were under the law, we could not come into the bonds of the new covenant, — the covenant of grace. But, through the death of Christ, we are dead to the law, and therefore we are set free from the principle and covenant of law, and we have come under the covenant of grace.

Romans 7:5. For when we were in the flesh, the motions of sins, which were by the law, did work in our members to bring forth fruit unto death.

Sin is the transgression of the law. Therefore, out of the law, by reason of our corruption, springs sin. And, in our past lives, we did indeed find sin to be very fruitful. It grew very fast in our members, and it brought forth much "fruit unto death."

Romans 7:6. But now we are delivered from the law, that being dead wherein we were held; that we should serve in newness of spirit, and not in the oldness of the letter.

No longer is the message to us, "This do, and thou shalt live." No more are we slaves under bondage; but we have come into a new state, we are free, rejoicing in the glorious liberty of the children of God; and what we now do is done out of a spirit of love, and not of fear. We are not seeking after holiness in order to be saved by it, neither do we seek to escape from sin because we are under any fear of being cast into hell. We have another spirit altogether within us.

Romans 7:7. What shall we say then? Is the law sin? God forbid.

Nay, so far from being sin, the law is the great detective of sin, discovering it, and letting us know what sin really is.

Romans 7:7-8. Nay, I had not known sin, but by the law: for I had not known lust, except the law had said, Thou shalt not covet. But sin, taking occasion by the commandment, wrought in me all manner of concupiscence.

Or, "covetousness." The very fact that God said to us, "Do it not," wrought upon our nature so that we wanted to do it, and that which God commanded, which was a matter of indifference to us while we were in ignorance of his will, became, by reason of the depravity of our hearts, a thing to be resisted just because he had enjoined it upon us. Ah, me! what wicked hearts are ours that fetch evil even out of good!

Romans 7:8-9. For without the law sin was dead. For I was alive without the law once: but when the commandment came, sin revived, and I died.

"I did not know how sinful I was until God's commandment came to me. Sin seemed to be dead within me, and I thought myself a righteous man; but when the law of God came home to my heart and conscience, and I understood that even a sinful thought would ruin me, that a hasty word had the essence of murder in it, and that the utmost uncleanness might lurk under the cover of what seemed a mere custom of my fellow-men, — when I found out all this, sin did indeed live, but I died so far as righteousness was concerned."

Romans 7:10-13. And the commandment, which was ordained to life, I found to be unto death. For sin, taking occasion by the commandment, deceived me, and by it slew me. Wherefore the law is holy, and the commandment holy, and just, and good. Was then that which is good made death unto me? God forbid.

"If I sinned the more when God's commandment was revealed to me; and if, by the light of the law, sin was made more apparent to me, and became so exceeding sinful that it drove me to despair, and so to commit still worse sin; the fault was not in the law, but in sin, and in me, the sinner."

Romans 7:13-14. But sin, that it might appear sin, working death in me by that which is good; that sin by the commandment might become exceeding sinful. For we know that the law is spiritual:

The law of the Lord is a far higher thing than it seems to be in the esteem of many people. Talk not of it as a mere "decalogue." It has far-reaching hands, and it affects the secret thoughts and purposes of men, and even their stray imaginations come under its supremacy. "The law is spiritual."

Romans 7:14. But I am carnal, sold under sin.

"I am carnal." There is the source of all the mischief, — a disobedient and rebellious subject, not an irksome law. The law is good enough, it is absolutely perfect; "but," says the apostle, "I am carnal," — fleshly, — "sold under sin."

Romans 7:15. For that which I do I allow not:

The man himself does that which is evil, but his conscience revolts against it.

Romans 7:15. For what I would, that do I not; but what I hate, that do I.

This is a strange contradiction, — a man who has grace enough to will to do good, and yet does it not. There are two men in the one man, — the new nature struggling against the old nature. This must be a renewed man who talks in this fashion, or else he could not say that he hated sin; yet there must be a part of him still imperfect, or else he would not do that which he hates.

Romans 7:16. If then I do that which I would not, I consent unto the law that it is good.

"If I do that against which and my conscience rebel, so far, the better part of me owns the goodness of the law, though the baser part of me rebels against it."

Romans 7:17. Now then it is no more I that do it, but sin that dwelleth in me.

The renewed man still stands out against sin. His heart is not wishful to sin, but that old nature within him will sin even to the end.

Romans 7:18-19. For I know that in me (that is, in my flesh,) dwelleth no good thing: for to will is present with me; but how to perform that which is good I find not. For the good that I would I do not: but the evil which I would not, that I do.

Oh, how often have men, who have been struggling after holiness, had to use these words of the apostle! The more holy they become, the more they realize that there is still a something better beyond them, after which they struggle, but to which they cannot yet attain; so still they cry, "The good that we would we do not: but the evil which we would not, that we do."

Romans 7:20. Now if I do that I would not, it is no more I that do it, but sin that dwelleth in me.

The true man — the newborn man — is struggling after that which is right. The real "I ", the immortal "ego", is still pressing forward, like a ship beating up against wind and tide, and striving to reach the harbor where it shall find perfect rest. Oh, what struggles, what contentions, what rightings, there are within the men and women in whom the grace of God is working mightily! Those who have but little grace can take things easily, and swim with the current; but where grace is mighty, sin will fight for the mastery, though it must yield ultimately, for there can never be any true peace until it is subdued.

Romans 7:21. I find then a law, that, when I would do good, evil is present with me.

Speaking for myself, I can say that, often, when I am most earnest in prayer, stray thoughts will come into my mind to draw me off from the holy work of supplication; and when I am most intently aiming at humility, then the shadow of pride falls upon me. Do not gracious men generally find it so? If their experience is like that of the apostle Paul, or like that of many another child of God whose biography one delights to read, it is so, and it will be so.

Romans 7:22-24. For I delight in the law of God after the inward man: but I see another law in my members, warring against the law of my mind, and bringing me into captivity to the law of sin which is in my members. O wretched man that I am! who shall deliver me from the body of this death?

These are birth-pangs, the throes and anguish of a regenerated spirit. The Christian man is fighting his way to sure and certain victory; so, the more of this wretchedness that he feels, the better, if it be only caused by a consciousness that sin is still lurking within him, and that he longs to be rid of it.

Romans 7:25. I thank God through Jesus Christ our Lord. So then with the mind I myself serve the law of God; but with the flesh the law of sin.

This exposition consisted of readings from Romans 7, and Romans 8:1-4.

Verses 7-25

This is Paul's own account of his inward conflicts. He longed to conquer sin. He wanted to become a free man, and live always a godly and holy life, but he found that there was a battle within his nature.

Romans 7:7. What shall we say then? Is the law sin? God forbid. Nay, I had not known sin, but by the law: for I had not known lust, except the law had said, Thou shalt not covet.

There are some who hope to overcome their evil propensities by the law. They think that if they can know and feel the authority of the law of God, that will have an awe over their minds, and they shall become holy. Now the law is in itself supremely holy. It cannot be improved. We could not add to it, or take from it without injuring it. It is a perfect law. But what is its effect upon the mind? When it comes into an unrenewed mind, instead of checking sin, it causes sin. The apostle says that he not known lust, except the law had said, "Thou shalt not covet." There is a something about us which rebels against law the moment we come to it. There are some things we should never think of doing if we were not prohibited from them, and then there becomes a tendency at once in this vile nature of ours to break the law.

Romans 7:8. But sin, taking occasion by the commandment, wrought in me all manner of concupiscence. For without the law sin was dead.

If there had never been any law, there could not have been any sin, because sin is a breaking of law. The law is good. We are not speaking about that. The law is necessary, but, still such is our nature that the very existence of law argues and creates the existence of sin. And when the law comes, then sin comes immediately. "Without the law sin was dead."

Romans 7:9. For I was alive without the law once;

I thought that I was everything that was good. I imagined that I was doing everything that was right. I felt no rebellion in my heart. I was alive.

Romans 7:9. But when the commandment came, sin revived, and I died.

I kicked at that commandment. My holiness was soon gone. The excellence which I thought I had in my character soon vanished for I found myself breaking the law.

Romans 7:10-13. And the commandment, which was ordained to life, I found to be unto death. For sin, taking occasion by the commandment, deceived me, and by it slew me. Wherefore the law is holy, and the commandment holy, and just, and good. Was then that which is good made death unto me? God forbid. But, sin, that it might appear sin, working death in me by that which is good: that sin by the commandment might become exceeding sinful.

There was sin in his nature, but he did not know it. But when the commandment came, then that evil nature said, "I won't keep that commandment," and it took occasion at once to show itself by breaking that commandment. It was something like a medicine which many a wise physician has given to his patient. There is a deadly disease in the internals of the man, and he gives him a medicine that throws it out. You see it on the skin. You feel the pain of it. It would have been his death anyhow. It can only be his death now; but now it is a part of the process of the cure to bring the disease where it can be seen. And so the law comes into a man's heart, and because of the rebellion of his nature, he kicks against the law and sins. It does not make him sinful. It only shows that he was sinful, for a perfect law would not make a perfect man sin. It would lead and guide him in the way of holiness. But a perfect law coming into contact with an imperfect nature soon creates rebellion and sin. It is an illustration that is not good throughout, but still it is of some use. You have seen quicklime; and you throw water on it. The water is of a cooling nature. There is nothing in the water but that which would quench fire, and yet when it is thrown upon the lime the consequence is a burning heat. So is it with the law cast upon man's nature. It seems to create sin. Not that the law does it of itself, but, coming into contact with the vicious principles of our nature, sin becomes the product of it. It is the only product. You may preach up the law of God till everybody becomes worse than he was before. You may read the ten commandments till men learn what to do in order to provoke God. The law does not create holiness. It never can.

Romans 7:14. For we know that the law is spiritual: but I am carnal,

Fleshly.

Romans 7:14. Sold under sin.

Even now that I have become a Christian and am renewed by grace.

Romans 7:15. For that which I do I allow not:

I often do that which I do not justify, which I do not wish to do again, which I abhor myself for doing.

Romans 7:16. For what I would, that do I not; but what I hate, that do I.

This is the believer's riddle. To say that this is not a believer's experience is to prove that the man who says it does not know much about how believers feel. We hate sin, and yet, alas! alas! we fall into it! We would live perfect lives if we could, we that are renewed. We make no justification for our sin: it is evil and abominable; yet do we find these two things warring and fighting within.

Romans 7:16. If then I do that which I would not, I consent unto the law that it is good.

My inmost heart, says the law, is good, though I have not kept it as I wish I had, yet my very wish to keep it is the consent of my nature to goodness of that law, and proves that there is a vitality about me which will yet throw out the disease, and make me right in the sight of God.

Romans 7:17. Now then it is no more I that do it,

The real "I," the true "I," the new-born "ego." Thank God for that—to have a will to do good, to have a strong, passionate desire to be holy. "To will is present with me."

Romans 7:17. But sin that dwelleth in me.

I would be earnest in prayer, and my thoughts are distracted. I would love God with all my heart, and something else comes in and steals away a part of it. I would be holy as God is holy, but I find myself falling short of my desires. So the apostle means.

Romans 7:18-20, For I know that in me (that is, in my flesh,) dwelleth no good thing: for to will is present with me: but how to perform that which is good I find not. For the good that I would I do not: but the evil which I would not that I do. Now if I do that I would not, it is no more I that do it,

The true and real "I."

Romans 7:20. But sin that dwelleth in me.

Oh! this accursed indwelling sin! Would God it were driven out. We do not say this to excuse ourselves-God forbid—but to blame ourselves that we permit this sin to dwell within us. Yet must we rejoice in God that we are born again, and that this new "I" the true "I," will not yield to sin, but fights against it.

Romans 7:21. I find then a law,

Or rule.

Romans 7:21-24. That, when I would do good, evil is present with me. For I delight in the law of God after the inward man: But I see another law in my members, warring against the law of my mind, and bringing me into captivity to the law of sin which is in my members. O wretched man that I am! who shall deliver me from the body of this death?

Now, the more holy a man gets the more he cries in this fashion. While he is low down in the scale, he puts up with sin, and he is uneasy, but when he gets to see Christ and get somewhat like him, the more nearly he approximates to the image of his Master, the more the presence of the least sinful thought is horrifying to him. He would, if he could, never look on sin again—never have the slightest inclination to it, but he finds his heart getting abroad and wandering when he would tether it down, if he could, to the cross and crucify it there. And so the more happy he is in Christ the more desperately does he cry against the wretchedness of being-touched with sin, even in the least degree. "Oh! wretched man that I am! Who shall deliver me from the body of this death?"

Romans 7:25. I thank God through Jesus Christ our Lord.

It will be done. I shall be delivered. I shall be perfect.
"Oh, blissful hour! oh, sweet abode!
I shall be near and like my God."
Oh! to be without fault before the throne, without tendency to sin without the possibility of it, immaculately clean, with a heart that sends forth pure waters like the river of life that flows from beneath the throne of God! This is our portion. We are looking for it, and we will never rest until we get it, blessed be his name. "I thank God through Jesus Christ our Lord."

Romans 7:25. So then with the mind I myself serve the law of God;

With the new mature.

Romans 7:25. But with the flesh the law of sin.

With the flesh—this old rubbishing stuff that must die and be buried, and the sooner the better. With my old corrupt nature I serve the law of sin. But what a mercy it is that the next verse is, that, notwithstanding that, "There is, therefore, now no condemnation to them which are in Christ Jesus, who walk not after the flesh but after the Spirit."

This exposition consisted of readings from Psalms 51. and Romans 7:7-25.

ROMANS 8

Verses 1-4

Romans 8:1. There is therefore now no condemnation to them which are in Christ Jesus, who walk not after the flesh, but after the Spirit.

Some people talk about "getting out of the 7th chapter, into the 8th." But who made this into an eighth chapter? Certainly, the Holy Spirit did not. There are no chapters in the Epistle as he inspired Paul to write it, the whole of it runs straight on without a break: "Therein therefore now no condemnation" — while struggling, fighting, warring, contending, —

Romans 8:2. For the law of the spirit of life in Christ Jesus hath made me free from the law of sin and death.

"Hath made me free" — that is, the real "I" of which he wrote a little while before — the true man himself: "' The law of the Spirit of life in Christ Jesus hath made me free from the law of sin and death.' I have broken its bonds, I am a free man. Contending against its usurpation, I have escaped from under its yoke, and I shall yet tread sin under my feet, and God shall bruise even Satan himself under my feet shortly."

Romans 8:3. For what the law could not do, in that it was weak through the flesh, God sending his own Son in the likeness of sinful flesh, and for sin, condemned sin in the flesh:

That he has done most effectually.

Romans 8:4. That the righteousness of the law might be fulfilled in us, who walk not after the flesh, but after the Spirit.

Oh, what a blessed thing it is to walk, freely, "not after the flesh, but after the Spirit" even though, all the while, there is, within the soul, this strife that the apostle has been describing!

This exposition consisted of readings from Romans 7, and Romans 8:1-4.

Verses 1-9

Romans 8:1. There is therefore now no condemnation to them which are in Christ Jesus, who walk not after the flesh, but after the Spirit.

My hearers, we are each of us, by nature, under the condemnation of God. We are not only subject to condemnation, but we are condemned already; and, on account of sin, there is judgment recorded in God's book against every one of us, considered in our fallen state. But if we "are in Christ Jesus," if we are made partakers of Jesus, if we have hidden ourselves in the cleft of the rock, Christ, and if our trust is solely in him, oh, precious thought, "there is therefore now no condemnation" for us. It is blotted out. The old judgment that was recorded against us is now erased; and in God's book of remembrance there is not to be found a single condemnatory syllable, nor one word of anger written against any believer in Christ Jesus. Glorious freedom from condemnation! How may I know whether I have been thus set free? This is the question that should enter into each of our hearts. The answer is: "Who walk not after the flesh, but after the Spirit." My hearers, after which of these are you and I walking? Are we following the flesh? Are we seeking to please ourselves, to indulge our bodies, to gratify our lusts, to satisfy our own inclinations? If so, we are not in Christ Jesus; for those who are in Christ Jesus "walk not after the flesh, but after the Spirit," and every one of you who is fleshly and carnal is not in Christ, but is still under condemnation.

Romans 8:2-3. For the law of the Spirit of life in Christ Jesus hath made me free from the law of sin and death. For what the law could not do, in that it was weak through the flesh, God sending his own Son in the likeness of sinful flesh, and for sin, condemned sin in the flesh:

He did accomplish it. The law could not condemn sin so truly and so thoroughly as God did when he condemned sin in the person of Christ. O believer, let not thy sins grieve thee,-however great or however tremendous they may have been; weep over them, but do not be distressed about them, for they have been condemned in Christ Jesus. They may have been enormous, but if thou art in him, Christ was punished for thee, and God's justice asks not for a second punishment for one offence. Christ offered once a complete atonement for all believers, and if I am a believer in him, there is no possible fear of my ever being condemned. There cannot be; for Christ was condemned for me, my sins were laid upon his head; and in the awful moment when he sustained the stroke of his Father's vengeance, those sins ceased to be; and "there is therefore now no condemnation to them which are in Christ Jesus."

Romans 8:4. That the righteousness of the law might be fulfilled in us, who walk not after the flesh, but after the Spirit.

Mark, again, how Paul brings us to this as the great evidence of our being in Christ Jesus,-the not walking after the flesh. Now, every man, as he is born into the world, left to himself, is sure to "walk after the flesh." It is only the man who has the Spirit of God put into his soul, who has the heavenly gift from on high, who will "walk after the Spirit." It is not talking after the flesh, but it is walking after it, that condemns us, and it is not talking after the Spirit that will save us, it is walking after the Spirit that is the evidence of salvation; not talking, but walking. How many of you are there who are talkatives, who can talk religion, and give us as much as we like of it, but whose life and conversation are not such as become godliness! "Be not deceived; God is not mocked: for whatsoever a man soweth, that shall he also reap." If ye sow to the flesh, ye "shall of the flesh reap corruption," but if ye sow to the Spirit, ye "shall of the Spirit reap life everlasting."

Romans 8:5-7. For they that are after the flesh do mind the things of the flesh; but they that are after the Spirit the things of the Spirit. For to be carnally minded is death; but to be spiritually minded is life and peace. Because the carnal mind is enmity against God:

That mind with which we are all born is enmity against God, and however much refined or polished a man may be, however amiable or polite, however he may shine amongst his fellow-creatures, if he has not had a new heart and a right spirit, he is at "enmity against God," and he cannot enter heaven until there has been a divine change wrought in him. Some of you suppose because you have never been guilty of any vice, because you have not indulged in any great transgression, that therefore you do not require the work of regeneration in your hearts. You will be mightily mistaken if you continue under that delusion until the last great day. "For to be carnally minded," even though that carnal mind is in a body that is dressed in silks and satins, "To be carnally minded is death," even though it be whitewashed till it looks like a spiritual one. "To be carnally minded," even though you sow the carnal mind with a few good garden seeds of the flowers of morality, will still be nothing but damnation to you at the last. "To be carnally minded is death;" only, "to be spiritually minded is life and peace. Because the carnal mind is enmity against God:"

Romans 8:7. For it is not subject to the law of God, neither indeed can be.

The opponents of the free-grace gospel, which it is our delight to preach, assert that men can be saved, if they will, and that men most certainly can repent, and can believe, and can come to God of their own free will, and that it is not through any defect in any powers that they have if they are not saved. Now, we are not over prone to controvert that point; but, at the same time, we do not understand the meaning of this verse if what they say is correct. It says here, "The carnal mind is not subject to the law of God, neither indeed can be." Some say that men could repent if it were their inclination. Exactly so; but that is what we assert,-that it never will be and never can be their inclination, except they are constrained to do so by the grace of God. Rowland Hill uses a very singular and odd metaphor in his "Village Dialogues." Two parties are speaking together on this subject, and one of them, pointing to the cat sitting on the hearth says, "Do you see that cat? She sits there, and licks her paws, and washes herself clean." "I see that," said the other. "Well," said the first speaker, "did you ever hear of one of the hogs taken out of the sty that did so?" "No," said he. "But he could if he liked," said the other. Ah, verily, he could if he liked; but it is not according to his nature, and you never saw such a thing done, and until you have changed the swine's nature, he cannot perform such a good action; and God's Word says the same of man. We do not care about fifty thousand aphorisms, or syllogisms, or anything else; God's Word against man's any day. Jesus said, "No man can come to me, except the Father which hath sent me draw him." "The carnal mind is enmity against God." Men cannot come to Jesus, unless the Father draws them to him. We assert that, from first to last, the work of salvation is all of grace; and we are not afraid of any licentious tendency of that doctrine, or anything of the kind. God's Word, in all its simplicity, must be preached, and we leave him to take care of his own truth. Blessed be God, this humbling truth is of far more use than the other doctrine, which puffs men up with pride, telling them that they can perform what most assuredly they cannot do. "It is not subject to the law of God, neither indeed can be."

Romans 8:8. So then they that are in the flesh cannot please God.

No man "in the flesh" can please God. Oh, what a sword this is,-a sharp two-edged sword against many of you, my friends! Some of you who regularly attend this house of prayer, and others of you who stray in here in the evening, you "are in the flesh," and you "cannot please God." Perhaps you have been attempting to do it. You have said, "I will attend the house of prayer regularly." You cannot please God by doing that, so long as you are "in the flesh." You may be as moral as you please, and we beseech you so to be; but unless you have the Spirit of God unless you are really changed in heart, and made new creatures in Christ Jesus, all that you can do, as long as you are "in the flesh, cannot please God." Virtues, in unregenerate men, are nothing but whitewashed sins. The best performance of an unchanged character is worthless in God's sight. It lacks the stamp of grace upon it; and that which has not the stamp of grace is false coin. Be it ever so beautiful in model and finish it is not what it should be. "So then they that are in the flesh cannot praise God."

Romans 8:9. But ye are not in the flesh, but in the Spirit, if so be that the Spirit of God dwell in you. Now if any may have not the Spirit of Christ, he is none of his.

O beloved, we have need each of us to put ourselves in this scale! Come, preacher, be not too sure of thine own salvation. Come, church-member, do not be too certain of thine own regeneration. Come, Christian, put thyself in this scale: "If any man have not the Spirit of Christ, he is none of his." If he has not the Holy Ghost really dwelling in him, guiding him, directing him, teaching him, comforting him, supporting him, he is none of Christ's. And if we do not exhibit the Spirit of Christ in our character,-if we have not gentleness, meekness, purity, holiness, benevolence, we are none of Christ's. Ah, this will take some of your flimsy Christians to pieces. Half of your professors, we fear, will at the last be found not to have had "the Spirit of Christ." It is one thing to profess religion, beloved, it is quite another thing to possess vital godliness. We may sit down at the communion table, but oh! if we never had the Spirit of Christ, we "are none of his." We may plead our own goodness before the throne of God at the last; but Jesus Christ will say, "You have not my Spirit; you are none of mine;" and then, however much we may have striven to serve God, unless we have the Spirit of Christ, there shall be nothing for us but the fearful curse, "Depart! depart! depart!" "O come, let us worship and bow down: let us kneel before the Lord our Maker." Let us ask him for his Spirit; let us plead with him for his grace; and though some of you have never had it, yet if you now ask for it, our God is a gracious God, full of mercy, and exceedingly pitiful; whosoever calleth upon his name shall be saved; and though the chief of sinners, if you sincerely ask for pardon and for grace, you shall receive it at his hand. The Lord help you so to pray, for Jesus Christ's sake! Amen.

This exposition consisted of readings from Psalms 66.; and Romans 8:1-9.

Verses 1-14

This wonderful chapter is the very cream of the cream of Holy Scripture. What a grand key-note the apostle strikes in the first verse!

Romans 8:1. There is therefore now no condemnation to them which are in Christ Jesus, who walk not after the flesh, but after the Spirit.

"No condemnation" — that is the first note of the chapter. In the last verse it is "no separation." What glorious music there is here, — no condemnation to those who are in Christ, no separation of them from Christ! Happy are the people who have a share in this double blessing, and unhappy are the men and women who know nothing of it. We will read it again: "There is therefore now no condemnation, "There is a great deal of accusation, and a great deal more of tribulation, but there is no condemnation not the least hint of it. Some condemnation we might have expected, but "there is therefore now no condemnation to them which are in Christ Jesus, who walk not after the flesh, but after the Spirit."

Romans 8:2. For the law of the Spirit of life in Christ Jesus hath made me free from the law of sin and death.

I have broken away from its thralldom; the new law, the law of the Spirit of life in Christ Jesus, the law of grace has set me free from the domination of the law of sin and death. Happy is the free man who is thus liberated by the grace of God.

Romans 8:3. For what the law could not do, —

God has done by his grace: " What the law could not do," —

Romans 8:3. In that it was weak through the flesh, God sending his own Son in the likeness of sinful flesh, and for sin, —

Or, as the marginal reading renders it, "by a sacrifice for sin," —

Romans 8:3-5. Condemned sin in the flesh: that the righteousness of the law might be fulfilled in us, who walk not after the flesh, but after the Spirit. For they that are after the flesh do mind the things of the flesh;

Unregenerate men, the men who remain in the state in which they were born, the men who allow their lower nature to have the predominance, "they that are after the flesh do mind the things of the flesh." That is all that they care about, all that they think about, all that they toil for, all that they really "mind."

Romans 8:5. But they that are after the Spirit the things of the Spirit.

Those in whom there is a new life begotten by the Holy Ghost — these mind the things of the Spirit. Each nature seeks its own things, — the flesh seeks the things of the flesh, the spirit seeks the things of the Spirit. Judge ye, my hearers, to which case ye belong by this test, — for what are you living? That which you live for is the true index of your nature. Do you mind spiritual things or the things of the flesh?

Romans 8:6-7. For to be carnally minded is death; but to be spiritually minded is life and peace. Because the carnal mind is enmity against God: for it is not subject to the law of God, neither indeed can be.

The old nature never will obey the law of God; it never can do so. What then is to be done with it? Improve it? Nay, my brethren, the only thing to be done with it is to let it die, and then to bury it. In baptism you have a most significant symbol of what is to be done with the flesh; you are to treat it as a dead thing, and therefore to bury it. Let the old life be crucified and put to death with Christ, and let the new life take its place.

Romans 8:8. So then they that are in the flesh —

Those who are still in the old nature, living for it, living to it, —

Romans 8:8. Cannot please God.

Men may wash this old nature, they may clothe it, they may decorate it, they may educate it, but there is no evolution which can produce grace out of nature. The child of nature may be finely dressed, but it is a dead child however gaudily it is attired. There is a vital eternal difference between the old nature and the new.

Romans 8:9. But ye are not in the flesh, but in the Spirit, if so be that the Spirit of God dwell in you.

Ye saints of Rome to whom Paul was writing, and ye who believe in Christ now: "Ye are not in the flesh, but in the Spirit, if so be that the Spirit of God dwell in you."

Romans 8:9. Now if any man have not the Spirit of Christ, he is none of his.

If Christ's Spirit has not quickened you, you do not belong to Christ. Some ministers preach a very general sort of gospel in which everybody has a share, but the Bible knows nothing of that sort of gospel. "If any man have not the Spirit of Christ, he is none of his." Do you know what it is to have the Spirit of Christ ? If not, my hearer, do not deceive yourself you are none of his. "If any man" — be he prince or magistrate, a member of Parliament or a doctor of divinity, — " if any man have not the Spirit of Christ, he is none of his."

Romans 8:10. And if Christ be in you, the body is dead because of sin; but the Spirit is life because of righteousness.

Hence the body suffers, the body is sick, the body decays, the body is under the dominion of death because of sin, but the Spirit is full of life because of righteousness.

Romans 8:11. But if the Spirit of him that raised up Jesus from the dead dwell in you, he that raised up Christ from the dead shall also quicken your mortal bodies by his Spirit that dwelleth in you.

You believers may have a good hope concerning your bodies: "He that raised up Christ from the dead shall also quicken your mortal bodies." Wait a while, therefore; what God has done for your souls he will in due time do for your bodies also. This should make you long for the day of Christ's appearing, as Paul says in the 23rd verse of this chapter, "waiting for the adoption, to wit, the redemption of our body," when Christ shall appear, and we shall be raised — "From beds of dust and silent clay," —the body itself born a second time, regenerate like the soul.

Romans 8:12. Therefore, brethren, we are debtors, not to the flesh, to live after the flesh.

We owe the flesh nothing; I mean the law of sin in our members, we owe nothing to that. It has been a curse and a plague to us; we are not debtors to the flesh, so we must not "live after the flesh."

Romans 8:13. For if ye live after the flesh, ye shall die:

If you live simply to gratify your ambition, if you live for avarice, if you live to please yourself, if you live for any earthly object which can be comprised under the term "after the flesh," you will certainly be disappointed, for you will die, and your hope will die with you.

Romans 8:13. But if ye through the spirit do mortify the deeds of the body, ye shall live.

If you seek, by the Holy Spirit's power, to kill sin, if you try to crush all sinful desires, if you keep evil with a rope about its neck, if you mortify it put it to death, then you shall live. Holiness is the mode of the Christian; life, sin is the way of the sinner's death

Romans 8:14. For as many as are led by the Spirit of God, they are the sons of God.

Verses 1-22

This precious chapter reminds us of the description of the land of Havilah, "where there is gold, and the gold of that land is good."

Romans 8:1. There is therefore now no condemnation to them which are in Christ Jesus,

There is no condemnation to them; that is gone, and gone for ever. Not only is part of it removed, but the whole of it is gone: "There is therefore now no condemnation to them which are in Christ Jesus." This is their legal status before God,—in Christ Jesus, without condemnation; and this is their character:—

Romans 8:1. Who walk not after the flesh, but after the Spirit.

Their daily conversation is according to their new spiritual nature, and according to the guidance of the Holy Spirit; and not according to their fleshly nature, and the guidance of self and Satan.

Romans 8:2. For the law of the Spirit of Life in Christ Jesus hath made me free from the law of sin and death.

"It cannot any longer rule me; and it cannot now condemn me. I am free from it, for I am now under the new and higher 'law of the Spirit of life in Christ Jesus."

Romans 8:3-4. For what the law could not do, in that it was weak through the flesh, God sending his own Son in the likeness of sinful flesh, and for sin, condemned sin in the flesh: that the righteousness of the law might be fulfilled in us, who walk not after the flesh, but after the Spirit.

If there are any men in the world who do keep the law of God, they are the very persons who do not hope to be saved by the keeping of it, for they have by faith found righteousness in Christ, aid now by love and gratitude are put under the power of the law of the spiritual life in Christ, and they so live, by God's grace, that they do manifest the holiness of the law in their lives.

Romans 8:5. For they that are after the flesh do mind the things of the flesh;

They care for nothing else: they are satisfied so long as their appetites are gratified. They are of this world, and the things of this world fill them to the brim.

Romans 8:5. But they that are after the Spirit the things of the Spirit.

Spiritual joys, spiritual hopes, spiritual pursuits,—these belong only to those who are spiritual.

Romans 8:6. For to be carnally minded—

To be fleshly minded

Romans 8:6. is death;

That is what it comes to, for the flesh comes to death at last; and, after death, it goes to corruption. If we live after that carnal fashion, this will be the end of our living: "death."

Romans 8:6. But to be spiritually minded is life and peace.

For the spirit will never die, and the spirit has that within it which will bring it perfect peace.

Romans 8:7-8. Because the carnal mind is enmity against God: for it is not subject to the law of God, neither indeed can be. So then they that are in the flesh cannot please God.

Those that have never been born again, so as to be "in the Spirit," are still just as they were born "in the flesh," so they cannot please God. Do what they may, there is an essential impurity about their nature so that they cannot be well pleasing unto God. We must be born again, we must become spiritual by the new birth which is wrought by the Holy Spirit, or else it is impossible for us to please God. O you who are trying your best to please God apart from the new birth, and apart from Christ, see how this iron bar is put across your path: "they that are in the flesh cannot please God." Go then to him, and ask him to give you of his Spirit, that you may be spiritual, and no longer carnal.

Romans 8:9. But ye are not in the flesh, but in the Spirit, if so be that the Spirit of God dwell in you. Now if any man have not the Spirit of Christ, he is none of his.

It does not matter what he calls himself; he may be a preacher, he may be a bishop; but if he has not the Spirit of Christ, "he is none of his;" and if he has the Spirit of Christ, though he may be the most obscure person on earth, he belongs to Christ.

Romans 8:10. And if Christ be in you, the body is dead because of sin;

The grace of God has not changed that body; it still remains earth, dust, worms' meat, and it must die unless Christ should come, and transform it by his coming. "The body is dead because of sin;" and hence come those aches and pains, that heaviness, that weariness, that decay, those infirmities of age which we experience so long as we bear about with us this body of death.

Romans 8:10. But the Spirit is life because of righteousness.

There is a living power within us which triumphs over this dying, decaying body. So we rejoice notwithstanding all our afflictions, trials, and depressions.

Romans 8:11. But if the Spirit of him that raised up Jesus from the dead dwell in you, he that raised up Christ from the dead shall also quicken your mortal bodies by his Spirit that dwelleth in you.

There is to be an emancipation even for this poor flesh, a translation and a glory for it yet in Christ.

Romans 8:12. Therefore, brethren, we are debtors, not to the flesh, to live after the flesh.

Certainly not, for we owe the flesh nothing. It keeps us down and hampers us, it is a hindrance to us, but we certainly owe it nothing; so let us not be subservient to it, let us not consult or even consider it, and especially let us never come under its fatal bondage.

Romans 8:13. For if ye live after the flesh, ye shall die:

It is a dying thing, and "ye shall die" if ye live after its dying fashion..

Romans 8:13. But if ye through the Spirit—

That living, immortal power—

Romans 8:13-14. Do mortify the deeds of the body, ye shall live. For as many as are led by the Spirit of God, they are the sons of God:

Oh, high dignity and blessed privilege! As soon as ever we get away from the dominion of the flesh, and come to be led by the Spirit of God, and so become spiritual men, we have the evidence that we are the sons of God, for "God is a Spirit," so his sons must be spiritual.

Romans 8:15. For ye have not received the spirit of bondage again to fear;

We did have it once, and it wrought some good effect upon us for the time being; when we were under the Law, we felt ourselves to be in slavery, and that made us go to Christ for liberty.

Romans 8:15. But ye have received the Spirit of adoption, whereby we cry, Abba, Father.

Oh, blessed, blessed state of heart to feel that now we are born into the family of God, and that the choice word which no slave might ever pronounce may now be pronounced by us, "Abba"! It is a child's word, such as a little child utters when first he opens his mouth to speak, and it runs the same both backwards and forwards, -AB-BA. Oh to have a childlike spirit that, in whatever state of heart I am, I may still be able to say, in the accents even of spiritual infancy," Abba, Father"!

Romans 8:16. The Spirit itself beareth witness with our spirit, that we are the children of God :

What better testimony can we have than that of these two witnesses, first of our own spirit, and then of the Holy Spirit himself, "that we are the children of God"? Note that this is not spoken concerning everybody. The doctrine of the universal Fatherhood of God in a doctrine of the flesh, and not of the Spirit; it is not taught anywhere in God's Word. This is a Fatherhood which relates only to those who are spiritual; we are born into it by the new birth, and brought into it by an act of grace in adoption. "Beloved, now are we the sons of God;" this is a special privilege that belongs only to those who are spiritual.

Romans 8:17-18. And if children, then heirs; heirs of God, and joint-heirs with Christ; if so be that we suffer with him, that we may be also glorified together. For I reckon that the sufferings of this present time are not worthy to be compared with the glory which shall be revealed in us.

Do we suffer now? Then let us wait for something better that is yet to come. Yes, we do suffer, and in this we are in accord with the whole creation of God, for the whole creation is just now, as it were, enduring birth pangs. There is something better coming; but, meanwhile, it is troubled and perplexed, moaning and groaning.

Romans 8:19-22. For the earnest expectation of the creature waiteth for the manifestation of the sons of God. For the creature was made subject to vanity, not willingly, but by reason of him who hath subjected the same in hope, because the creature itself also shall be delivered from the bondage of corruption into the glorious liberty of the children of God. For we know that the whole creation groaneth and travaileth in pain together until now.

See how it often weeps in the superabundant rain that seems like a minor deluge. Note how, at times, creation's very bowels seem to be tossed and torn with pain and agony by volcanoes and earthquakes. Mark the tempests, tornadoes, hurricanes, and all kinds of ills that sweep over the globe, leaving devastation in their track; and the globe itself is wrapped in swaddling bands of mist, and shines not out like its sister stars in its pristine brightness and splendour. The animal creation, too, wears the yoke of bondage. How unnecessarily heavy have men often made that yoke!

Verses 1-31

Romans 8:1. There is therefore now no condemnation to them which are in Christ Jesus, who walk not after the flesh, but after the Spirit.

To my mind one of the sweetest words of that verse is that little word now.
"There is, therefore, now no condemnation" — at this very moment. Walking under the power of the Spirit of God in Christ Jesus, there is, therefore, now no condemnation to believers. It is a logical conclusion, too, from something that went before. You and I are not absolved from sin apart from the truth, but there is a great truth at the back of it which necessitates it. "There is, therefore, now no condemnation to them which are in Christ Jesus, who walk not after the flesh, but after the Spirit."

Romans 8:2. For the law of the Spirit of life in Christ Jesus hath made me free from the law of sin and death.

Sin and death cannot govern me — cannot condemn me — cannot destroy me. Another law has come in. The Spirit of life in Christ Jesus has brought me into another kingdom wherein I cannot be affected, so as to condemn me, by the law of sin and death.

Romans 8:3-4. For what the law could not do, in that it was weak through the flesh, God sending his own Son in the likeness of sinful flesh, and for sin, condemned sin in the flesh: That the righteousness of the law might be fulfilled in us, who walk not after the flesh, but after the Spirit.

The law of God was a good law, a just and holy law. It was weak, not in itself, for, verily, if righteousness could have been by any law, it would have been by the law of God. But it was weak through our flesh. We could not keep it. We could not fulfill the conditions of life laid down under it. Therefore, what the law could not do, God has now done for us. He has found a way of making us righteous through the righteousness of his own dear Son, whom he has sent in the likeness of sinful flesh. He has found out a way of condemning sin, without condemning us. He condemned sin in the flesh, but we escaped. And he has found out a way of making us practically righteous, too, through the abundance of his grace, enabling us to walk no longer after the flesh, but after the Spirit. Blessed be God for this, for when we had broken his law, he might justly have left us to take the consequences; but he has stepped aside: he has gone beyond all that might have been expected of him, and brought in a law by which a remedy is applied to all our ills. Glory be to his name!

Romans 8:5. For they that are after the flesh do mind the things of the flesh;

They live to eat and drink. They live for self-aggrandizement. They live for the world and its pleasures alone. It is according to their nature. Everything acts according to its nature. The wolf devours; the sheep patiently feeds. They that are after the flesh do mind the things of the flesh.

Romans 8:5. But they that are after the Spirit the things of the Spirit.

God has given us, then, the Spirit to dwell in us, and now I trust we can say that we desire holiness, and righteousness, and peace, and joy, in the Holy Ghost, for these things are the things of the Spirit.

Romans 8:6-7. For to be carnally minded is death; but to be spiritually minded is life and peace. Because the carnal mind is enmity against God: for it is not subject to the law of God, neither indeed can be.

It is so deeply vitiated, so thoroughly depraved, that so long as the fleshly mind exists, it will be in rebellion against God. "Ye must be born again," for that which is born of the flesh is flesh, and only that which is born of the Spirit is spirit. Unless we are renewed, then, by the Spirit of God, we never shall be subject to the law of God; neither, indeed, can we be.

Romans 8:8-9. So then they that are in the flesh cannot please God. But ye are not in the flesh, but in the Spirit, if so be that the Spirit of God dwell in you. Now if any man have not the Spirit of Christ, he is none of his.

Christ does not own any that are not indwelt by his Spirit. They may wear the Christian name; they may perform some acts which look like Christian acts; but all this avails nothing. You must have the Spirit of God within you, or else you are none of his; and what a thing it is to be "none of his." "Verily," says Christ, "I never knew you." "But, Lord, we ate and drank with thee: thou didst preach in our streets." But he says, "I never knew you." They are none of his. Oh! dear friends, the highest point to which human nature can reach of itself falls short of being in Christ. There must be the Spirit of God dwelling in us, or else we are none of his.

Romans 8:10. And if Christ be in you, the body is dead because of sin;

Therefore, it suffers disease and pain, for the soul is regenerated, but not the body. If I may so speak, the regeneration of the body happens at the resurrection. It is then that it will receive its full share of the blessed work of Christ. "The body is dead because of sin."

Romans 8:10-11. But the Spirit is life because of righteousness. But if the Spirit of him that raised up Jesus from the dead dwell in you, he that raised up Christ from the dead shall also quicken your mortal bodies by his Spirit that dwelleth in you.

So there is a complete deliverance provided for body, soul, and spirit. As Moses said to Pharaoh when he agreed to let the people of Israel go, but said that they must leave behind their flocks, "Not a hoof shall be left behind," so no particle of our real manhood shall be left under the thraldom of sin and death. The soul is already emancipated, and the body shall be, by the Spirit which dwells in you.

Romans 8:12. Therefore, brethren, we are debtors, not to the flesh, to live after the flesh.

For we owe the flesh nothing by way of gratitude or service. The flesh has dragged us down. The flesh has ruined us. We owe it nothing, except mastery of it. We are not debtors to it, to live after it.

Romans 8:13. For if ye live after the flesh, ye shall die:

It will die, and so will you, who make it your master.

Romans 8:13. But if ye through the Spirit do mortify the deeds of the body, ye shall live.

"Mortify," kill, put to death.

Romans 8:14. For as many as are led by the Spirit of God, they are the Sons of God.

There may be a great many weaknesses and infirmities about them, but if they follow the divine leadership of the Spirit of God, they are the sons of God.

Romans 8:15. For ye have not received the spirit of bondage again to fear; but ye have received the Spirit of adoption, whereby we cry Abba, Father.

Is this true of you? "Ye have received the Spirit of adoption, whereby we cry, Abba, Father." Dear friends, hearing these words, can you respond to them? Are they true of you?

Romans 8:16. The Spirit itself beareth witness with our spirit, that we are the children of God:

Many of you make a profession of being the children of God. Can your own spirit say that it is true? And is there, in addition to the witness of the Spirit within you that it is true? If not, unless there is a witness to our testimony, it avails nothing. Our Lord Jesus Christ said, "If I bear witness of myself, my witness is not true"; and if he chooses to put himself on a level, as it were, with the rest of humanity in that respect, we cannot expect that our witness will stand for ought if it stands alone. No, there must be the Spirit himself bearing witness with our spirit that we are the children of God.

Romans 8:17. And if children, then heirs: heirs of God, and joint-heirs with Christ;

Oh that if — "if children." There are some that get over all that. They believe in a universal fatherhood, which is not worth the words in which they describe it. This is a different fatherhood altogether.

Romans 8:17. If so be that we suffer with him, that we may be also glorified together.

Oh! this blessed co-partnership — this fellowship: joint-heirs with Christ: taking part in the whole heritage — as well the heritage of suffering as the heritage of glory. "It shall bruise thy heel, but thou shalt bruise his head." There is to be the heel-bruising for the Christ, as well as for us; but there is to be the head-crushing of sin and Satan for him and for us, too.

Romans 8:18. For I reckon that the sufferings of this present time are not worthy to be compared with the glory which shall be revealed in us.

Glory in us! Only think of that! You know the revelation that is in the book; but how grand will be the revelation that is in the man! "The glory which shall be revealed in us." We shall be full of glory. And a part of God's glory, which otherwise must have lain concealed, will be revealed in his people to his own praise forever and ever; but also to our own eternal joy.

Romans 8:19. For the earnest expectation of the creature waiteth for the manifestation of the sons of God.

There is something that the whole creation is waiting for, and it cannot come, till God's children are manifested — till the glory is revealed in them.

Romans 8:20-22. For the creation was made subject to vanity, not willingly, but by reason of him who hath subjected the same in hope. Because the creation itself also shall be delivered from the bondage of corruption into the glorious liberty of the children of God. For we know that the whole creation groaneth and travaileth in pain together until now.

"The whole creation." It is the same word all through; so I have put the same word. The whole world is in its pangs and birth-throes, and there can never come its complete deliverance into the new heavens and the new earth, except there shall also be the manifestation of the children of God, and their deliverance from all that now hampers and hinders the divine life that is within them.

Romans 8:23. And not only they, but ourselves also, which have the first fruits of the Spirit, even we ourselves groan within ourselves, waiting for the adoption, to wit, the redemption of our body.

This is what we are looking for. Our manhood is not all soul: it is body, too. And here, as yet, this poor body seems to lie outside the gate, like Lazarus, while the soul rejoices in God. But its time of glorifying is coming. The trump of the archangel shall proclaim it.

Romans 8:24. For we are saved by hope:

As yet we are saved by hope.

Romans 8:24-26. But hope that is seen is not hope: for what a man seeth, why doeth he yet hope for? But if we hope for that we see not, then do we with patience wait for it. Likewise the Spirit also helpeth our infirmities: for we know not what we should pray for as we ought: but the Spirit itself maketh intercession for us with groanings which cannot be uttered.

That is a grand thing. We have got the first-fruits of the Spirit to be the pledge of all the glorious harvest. The very fact that the Spirit dwells in us is the conclusive proof that our bodies shall be raised from the dead. Meanwhile, the Spirit of God is helping us, as we groan and labour, towards the complete perfection. "The Spirit helpeth our infirmities."

Romans 8:27. And he that searcheth the hearts knoweth what is the mind of the Spirit, because he maketh intercession for the saints according to the will of God.

Nor is it only the Holy Spirit who is thus helping us onward towards the grand finale.

Romans 8:28-29. And we know that all things work together for good to them that love God, to them who are the called according to his purpose. For whom he did foreknow, he also did predestinate to be conformed to the image of his Son, that he might be the firstborn among many brethren.

And you know that he is the first-born in this sense — not only as the greatest, but that as the first-begotten from among the dead, he has risen from the dead. He has risen from the dead, and in this he leads the way for us all. "That he might be the first-born among many brethren."

Romans 8:30. Moreover whom he did predestinate, them he also called: and whom he called, them he also justified: and whom he justified, them he also glorified.

No slips, no gaps or chasms, by the way. The foreknown are predestinated: the predestinated are the called: the called are justified: the justified are glorified.

Romans 8:31. What shall we then say to these things?

Shall we succumb under the sufferings of the body? Shall we yield to doubt because of all our heavy feelings, and the dullness that comes of the flesh? By no manner of means.

Romans 8:31. If God be for us, who can be against us? He that spared not his own Son, but delivered him up for us all, how shall he not with him also freely give us all things?

We can get through all these difficulties, if God be with us.

Verses 1-32

Romans 8:1. There is therefore now no condemnation to them which are in Christ Jesus, —

Observe that Paul writes "There is therefore," for he is stating a truth which is founded upon solid argument. "There is therefore now" — at this very day, at this very moment, — "no condemnation" — none of any sort, — none that will lie in the Court of Conscience or in the Court of King's Bench above: "There is therefore now no condemnation to them which are in Christ Jesus." Our forefathers used to read this verse, "There is therefore now no damnation." One of the martyrs, being brought before a Popish bishop, the bishop said to him, "Dying in thy heresy, thou wilt be damned." "That I never shall be," answered the good man, "for there is therefore now no damnation to them which are in Christ Jesus.'" He had sought the very spirit of the text, for there is nothing that can condemn the man who is in Christ Jesus.

Romans 8:1. Who walk not after the flesh, but after the Spirit.

This is the distinctive mark of a man in Christ Jesus. He does not let the flesh govern him, but the Spirit. The spiritual nature has come to the front, and the flesh must go to the back. The Spirit of the living God has entered into him, and become the master-power of his life. He walks "not after the flesh, but after the Spirit."

Romans 8:2. For the law of the Spirit of life in Christ Jesus hath made me free from the law of sin and death.

And nothing else can do that. Every man is, by nature, under bondage to that which Paul describes as "the law of sin and death." There is a law in our nature, which is so powerful that, even when we would do good, evil is present with us, and we cannot get away from that law, except by introducing another, which is "the law of the Spirit of life in Christ Jesus," Dr. Chalmers has a remarkable sermon upon it. The Expulsive Power of a New Affection;" and it is this new affection for Christ, which is the accompaniment of the new life in Christ, which expels the old forces that used to hold us under bondage to sin and death.

Romans 8:3-4. For what the law could not do, in that it was weak through the flesh, God sending his own Son in the likeness of sinful flesh, and for sin, condemned sin in the flesh: that the righteousness of the law might be fulfilled in us who walk not after the flesh, but after the Spirit.

The law never made anybody holy, and it never will do so. The law says to a man, "This is what you ought to do, and you will be condemned if you do not do it." That is quite true, but the law supplies no power to enable us to do this. It says to the lame man, "You must walk," and to the blind man, "You must see; "but it does not enable them either to walk or to see. On the contrary, our nature is such that, when the law issues its commands, there is a tendency in us at once to disobey them. There are some sins, which we never should have thought of committing if we had not been commanded not to do them, so that the law — not because of its own nature, but because of the wickedness of our nature, is weak and ineffectual for the producing of righteousness. But the Lord Jesus Christ has come, has lived, and has died, — died for us who are his people, and has put away our sins. Now we love him; now, being delivered from all condemnation, we love him who has delivered us, and this becomes the forge by which we are inclined to holiness, and led us further and further in a course, not merely of morality, but of holiness before God. What a blessed system this is, which saves the sinner from the love of sin, delivers a man from sinning, gives him a new nature, and puts a right spirit within him!

Romans 8:5. For they that are after the flesh do mind the things of the flesh;

Flesh cares for flesh. The man who is all body cares only for the body. The man, whose mind is under subjection to his body, minds "the things of the flesh."

Romans 8:5. But they that are after the Spirit the things of the Spirit.

Where the Holy Ghost is Supreme where the spiritual world has become predominant over the heart and life. There, men live for something nobler than the worldly man's trinity, "What shall we eat, and what shall we drink, and wherewithal shall we be clothed?" The carnal life is only becoming to a beast, or a bird, or an insect. But when a man cares for his immortal spirit, and lives for divine and spiritual things, he has attained to the life that is life indeed.

Romans 8:6-7. For to be carnally minded is death; but to be spiritually minded is life and peace. Because the carnal mind is enmity against God: for it is not subject to the law of God, neither indeed can be.

As long as a man lives only for this present evil world, lives for self, lives under the domination of the flesh, he cannot really know God, or truly serve him. Such a mind as his "is not subject to the law of God, neither indeed can be."

Romans 8:8. So then they that are in the flesh —

That is, those who are under its condemnation and power —

Romans 8:8-10. Cannot please God. But ye are not in the flesh, but in the Spirit, if so be that the Spirit of God dwell in you. Now if any man have not the Spirit of Christ, he is none of his. And if Christ be in you, the body is dead because of sin; but the Spirit is life because of righteousness.

So that although Christ dwells in a man, he must not reckon that he will be free from suffering, and pain, and sickness, for the body has not yet risen from the dead, and does not yet feel the full effect of regeneration. The soul is risen from the dead by regeneration, and it therefore "is life because of righteousness;" and the body will, in due time, also share in the power of Christ's Spirit. The day draweth near when we "shall be delivered from the bondage of corruption, into the glorious liberty of the children of God."

Romans 8:11-12. But if the Spirit of him that raised up Jesus from the dead dwell in you, he that raised up Christ from the dead shall also quickens your mortal bodies by his Spirit that dwelleth in you. Therefore, brethren, we are debtors, not to the flesh, to live after the flesh.

We have got nothing good out of the flesh at present, for it is not yet "delivered from the bondage of corruption," though it is to be delivered.

Romans 8:13. For if ye live after the flesh, ye shall die:

For the flesh is to die.

Romans 8:13. But if ye through the Spirit do mortify —

Or, kill —

Romans 8:13. The deeds of the body, ye shall live.

Shall a dying body, then, be my master? Shall the appetite for eating and drinking, or anything else that comes of the flesh, dominate my spirit? God forbid! Let death go to death, and the flesh is such; but the newly-given spirit of God, the spirit who has quickened us with immortal life shall rule and reign in us evermore.

Romans 8:14-21. For as many as are led by the Spirit of God, they are the sons of God. For ye have not received the spirit of bondage again to fear, but ye have received the Spirit of adoption, whereby we cry, Abba, Father. The Spirit itself beareth witness with our spirit, that we are the children of God. And if children, then heirs, heirs of God, and joint-heirs with Christ; if so be that we suffer with him, that we may be also glorified together.

For I reckon that the sufferings of the present time are not worthy to be compared with the glory which shall be revealed anew. For the earnest expectation of the creature waiteth for the manifestation of the Son of God. For the creature was made subject to vanity, not willingly, but by reason of him who hath subjected the same in hope. Because the creature itself also shall be delivered from the bondage of corruption into the glorious liberty of the children of God. We are part and parcel of creation, and we shall draw it along with us. There shall be new heavens and a new earth. The curse shall be taken from the garden, thorns and thistles shall no longer grow there; and there shall be no killing or devouring in all God's holy mountain. The galling yoke, which we have laid on the whole of creation by our sin, shall be taken off from it by our Redeemer.

Romans 8:22-23. For we know that the whole creation groaneth and travaileth in pain together until now. And not only they, but ourselves also, which have the first fruits of the Spirit, even we ourselves groan within ourselves, waiting for the adoption, to wit, the redemption of our body.

We groan in unison with a groaning creation, and we shall not at present get rid of our aches, and pains, and sicknesses altogether.

Romans 8:24-32. For we are saved by hope: but hope that is seen is not hope: for what a man seeth, why doth he yet hope for? But if we hope for that we see not, then do we with patience wait for it? Likewise the Spirit also helpeth our infirmities: for we know not what we should pray for as we ought: but the Spirit itself maketh intercession for us with groanings which cannot be uttered. And he that searcheth the heart knoweth what is the mind of the Spirit, because he maketh intercession for the saints according to the will of God. And we know that all things work together for good to them that love God, to them who are the called according to his purpose. For whom he did foreknow, he also did predestinate to be conformed to the image of his Son, that he might be the firstborn among many brethren. Moreover whom he did predestinate, them he also called: and whom he called, them he also justified: and whom he justified, them he also glorified. What shall we then say to these things? If God be for us, who can be against us? He that spared not his own Son, but delivered him up for us all, how shall he not with him also freely give us all things?

This exposition consisted of readings from Romans 3:9-27; Romans 5:6-11; Romans 8:1-32.

<u>Verses 1-34</u>

The words we are about to read follow a passage in which the Apostle describes the conflict of his soul. It is rather singular that it should be so.

To catch the contrast, let us just begin at the end of the 7th chapter, 22nd verse.

Romans 7:22-25 and **Romans 8:1**. For I delight in the law off God alter the inward man: But I see another law in my members, warring against the law of my mind, and bringing me into captivity to the law of sin which is in my members. O wretched man that I am! who shall deliver me from the body of this death? I thank God through Jesus Christ our Lord. So then with the mind I myself serve the law of God; but with the flesh the law of sin. There is therefore now no condemnation to them which are in Christ Jesus, who walk not after the flesh, but after the Spirit.

Some simpletons have said that Paul was not a converted man when he wrote the closing verses of that 7th chapter. I venture to assert that nobody but an advanced Christian, enjoying the highest degree of sanctification could ever have written it. It is not a man that is dead in sin that calls himself "wretched," because he finds sin within him; it is a man made pure by the grace of God, who, because of that very purity, tools more the comparatively lesser force of sin than he would have done when he had less grace and more sin. I believe that the nearer we get to absolute perfection, the more fit to enter the gates of heaven, the more detestable will sin become to us, and the more conflict will there be in our souls to tread out the last spark of sin. Bless God, beloved! if you feel a conflict, bless him and ask him that it may rage more terrible still, for that shall be one evidence to you that you are indeed out of all condemnation because you are struggling against the evil.

Romans 8:2. For the law of the Spirit of life in Christ Jesus hath made me free from the law of sin and death.

I am not the bond-slave of it; I am the enemy of it; I am free from it, fighting against it, struggling like a free man against one who would bring him into captivity; but even though I sometime feel as if I were a captive, I know I am not, I am free.

Romans 8:3-4. For what the law could not do, in that it was weak through the flesh, God sending his own Son in the likeness of sinful flesh, and for sin, condemned sin in the flesh: That the righteousness of the law might be fulfilled in us, who walk not niter the flesh, but after the Spirit.

This is our victory, that let the flesh lust as it may, we do not walk after it; we are kept by God's grace; we are preserved, so that the bent and tenor of our life is after the rule of the Spirit of God.

Romans 8:5-6. For they that are after the flesh do mind the things of the flesh; but they that are after the Spirit the things of the Spirit. For to be carnally minded is death; but to be spiritually minded is life and peace.

Oh! what a death it is to us if ever the flesh gets the mastery; and if it had the mastery in us, we should know that we were in death still; but oh! what a joy, what life, what peace it is to have the Spirit ruling in us, so that we are spiritually minded. God give us this to the full!

Romans 8:7-8. Because the carnal mind is enmity against God: for it is not subject to the law of God, neither indeed can be. So then they that are in the flesh cannot please God.

We must be born again then. It is no use improving the flesh. The taking away of the filth of the flesh was the old law, but the burying of the flesh, that is the new. The plunging of it into the death of Christ is the very sign of the new covenant. Oh! to know to the full, the power of the life of God for the death of the flesh!

Romans 8:9-10. But ye are not in the flesh, but in the Spirit, if so be that the Spirit of God dwell in you. Now if any man have not the Spirit of

Christ, he is none of his. And if Christ be in you, the body is dead because off sin; but the Spirit is life because of righteousness.

That is why we have aches and pains, and infirmities, because the body is dead; that is, doomed to die, must die; it must see corruption unless the Lord come, and even in that case it must undergo a wondrous change; so we regard our body as dead. No wonder, then, that all those aches and pains and troubles of body do come upon us. The day shall come when, however, even it shall be delivered from the power of death; meanwhile, blessed be God, "the Spirit is life because of righteousness."

Romans 8:11. But if the Spirit of him that raised up Jesus from the dead dwell in you, he that raised up Christ from the dead shall also quicken your mortal bodies by his Spirit that dwelleth in you.

The blessing of life is to come to the body too; it shall be immortal by-and-bye, delivered from all the infirmities and sorrows which sin and death have brought upon it.

Romans 8:12-13. Therefore, brethren, we are debtors, not to the flesh, to live after the flesh. For if ye live after the flesh, ye shall die: but if ye through the Spirit do mortify the deeds of the body, ye shall live.

It is a live thing, and a quickening thing, for ye shall live.

Romans 8:14. For as many as are led by the Spirit of God, they are the sons of God.

God has not got a dead child; never had one. God is not the God of the dead, but of the living.

Romans 8:15. For ye have not received the spirit of bondage again to fear; but ye have received the Spirit of adoption, whereby we cry, Abba, Father.

First, love, and then sonship; he rises in his strain.

Romans 8:16. The Spirit itself beareth witness with our spirit, that we are the children of God.

It is first a quickening spirit, and then a witnessing spirit, witnessing with our spirit that we are the children of God. Now up again.

Romans 8:17. And if children, then heirs; heirs of God, and joint-heirs with Christ; if so be that we suffer with him,

Up again: —

Romans 8:17. That we may be also glorified together.

Oh! what a rise is this from groaning under, "O wretched man that I am! Who shall deliver me from the body of this death?" up to this point, "That we may be also glorified together."

Romans 8:18-19. For I reckon that the sufferings of this present time are not worthy to be compared with the glory which shall be revealed in us. For the earnest expectation of the creature waiteth for the manifestation of the sons of God.

It is not merely that the Spirit will bless the body, but that spiritual men will bless the whole creation. Materialism, which is like the body inhabited by the spirits of saints, is to share in the bliss which Christ has come to bring.

Romans 8:20-22. For the creature was made subject to vanity, not willingly, but by reason of him who hath subjected the same in hope, Because the creature itself also shall be delivered from the bondage of corruption into the glorious liberty of the children of God. For we know that the whole creation groaneth and travaileth in pain together until now.

Just as our body is, so to speak, the world, the earth in which our spirit dwells: so this big earth is the body in which the Church dwells; and this body has its pains, so this creation has its pains; but as this body is to rise again, so this creation also, though it "groaneth and travaileth," is to be brought into the "glorious liberty of the children of God." And What a world it will be when the curse that fell on it through the sin of Eden shall be removed by the glorious Atonement of Calvary; and when the blood of Christ which fell to the ground, which you will remember has never gone away from the earth, but is somewhere still, shall have fully redeemed the world, the whole world shall be a trophy of the Redeemer's power.

Romans 8:23. And not only they, but ourselves also, which have the first fruits of the Spirit, even we ourselves groan within ourselves, waiting for the adoption, to wit, the redemption of our body.

Of course, we do groan within ourselves. Who said. we did not? And those brethren who say they never groan, I wish they would learn better. It is one of the signs of grace and marks of a child of God that he is not perfect, and does not think he is, but groans after it, cries after it. "We groan without ourselves, waiting for the adoption, to wit, the redemption of our body." For this poor body still lies in measure under a curse, still with its pains, still with its carnal appetites and fleshly tendencies to hamper and to trouble it, but this we groan after — that this flesh of ours, and the whole creation in which we dwell, shall yet have a joyous deliverance.

Romans 8:24-30. For we are saved by hope: but hope that is seen is not hope: for what a man seeth, why doth he yet hope for? But if we hope for that we see not, then do we with patience wait for it. Likewise the Spirit also helpeth our infirmities: for we know not what we should pray for as we ought: but the Spirit itself maketh intercession for us with groanings which cannot be uttered. And he that searcheth the hearts knoweth what is the mind of the Spirit, because he maketh intercession for the saints according to the will of God. And we know that all things work together for good to them that love God, to them who are the called according to his purpose. For whom he did foreknow, he also did predestinate to be conformed to the image of his Son, that he might be the firstborn among many brethren. Moreover whom he did predestinate, them he also called: and whom he called, them he also justified: and whom he justified, them he also glorified.

He speaks as if it were all done, because the major part of it is done in the saints, and it will only be a wink of the eye and it will all be done in every one of us who are believers. Let us look at it as done quite fully, even now, by hope that we are already glorified together.

Romans 8:31-32. What shall we then say to these things? If God be for us, who can be against us? He that spared not his own Son, but delivered him up for us all, how shall he not with him also freely give us all things!

What, indeed, what can we say? We are lost in wonder, love, and praise. Thus much, however, we can say, for it concerns our struggles while we are here below. Paul has got that shadow still ever him — of struggling against the flesh. What shall we say in the view of these blessed things concerning that struggle? Why, this: "If God be for us, Who can be against us?"

Romans 8:33-34. Who shall lay anything to the charge of God's elect? It is God that justifieth. Who is he that condemneth? It is Christ that died, yea rather, that is risen again, who is even at the right hand of God, who also maketh intercession for us.

Equally impossible; and if neither God nor Christ will condemn, what judge have we to fear? The Judge of all the earth, and the Judge of the quick and the dead — if neither of these condemn, condemn away who likes.

Verses 1-39

Romans 8:1. There is therefore now no condemnation to them which are in Christ Jesus, who walk not after the flesh, but after the Spirit.

"No condemnation": that is the beginning of the chapter. No separation: that is the end of the chapter. And all between is full of grace and truth. What a banquet this chapter has often proved to the souls of God's hungry servants! May it be so now as we read it. No condemnation even now. Many doubts, but no condemnation. Many chastisements, but no condemnation. Even frowns from the Father's face apparently, but no condemnation. And this is not a bare statement, but an inference from powerful arguments. "There is, therefore, now no condemnation to them which are in Christ Jesus." This is where they are. "Who walk not after the flesh, but after the Spirit." This is how they behave themselves, not under the government of the old nature, but under the rule of the divine Spirit of God.

Romans 8:2-4. For the law of the Spirit of life in Christ Jesus hath made me free from the law of sin and death. For what the law could not do, in that it was weak through the flesh, God sending his own Son in the likeness of sinful flesh, and for sin, condemned sin in the flesh: That the righteousness of the law might be fulfilled in us, who walk not after the flesh but after the Spirit.

None keep the law so well as those who do not hope to be saved by it, but who, renouncing all confidence in their own works, and accepting the righteousness which is of God by faith in Christ Jesus, are moved by gratitude to a height of consecration and a purity of obedience which mere legalism can never know. The child will obey better without desire of reward, than the slave will under the dread of the lash, or in hope of a wage. The most potent motive for holiness is free grace. A dying Saviour is the death of sin. As we have been singing, we strove against its power until we learnt that Christ was the way, and then we conquered it.

Romans 8:5. For they that are after the flesh do mind the things of the flesh; but they that are after the Spirit the things of the Spirit.

Everything according to its nature. Water will rise as high as its source, but it will not naturally flow any higher. The great thing, then, is to be brought under the dominion of the Holy Spirit, and of that new nature which is the offspring of the Spirit. Then we try to rise up to our source, and we rise vastly higher than human nature ever can under any force that you can apply to it. The new nature can do what the old nature cannot do.

Romans 8:6. For to be carnally minded

To have the mind of the flesh.

Romans 8:6. Is death; but to be spiritually minded is life and peace.

Flesh must die. Its tendency is to corruption; but the spirit never dies. Its tendency, its instinct, is growth, advance, immortality.

Romans 8:7. Because the careful mind is enmity against God: for it is not subject to the law of God, neither indeed can be.

The old nature is hopelessly bad. There is no mending it. It is enmity, not merely at enmity; but it is absolutely enmity. It is not subject to God's law, and you cannot make it so.

Romans 8:8. So then they that are in the flesh cannot please God.

So long as we are under the dominion of the old nature, the depraved and-fallen nature, there is no pleasing God.

Romans 8:9. But ye are not in the flesh, but in the Spirit, if so be that the Spirit of God dwell in you.

Oh! this is a very wonderful fact, that the Spirit of God should dwell in us. I have often said to you that I never know which of two mysteries most to admire — God incarnate in Christ, or the Holy Spirit indwelling in man; they are two marvelous things, miracles of miracles.

Romans 8:9-10. Now if any man have not the Spirit of Christ, he is none of his. And if Christ be in you, the body is dead because of sin; but the Spirit is life because of righteousness.

The regeneration of the body, so to speak, is not performed in this life; Resurrection is tantamount to that. The body is still under the old law of death, and so we have pain and weakness, and we die; but the spirit, oh! how it triumphs, even in the midst of pain and weakness. "The Spirit is life, because of righteousness." That will not die.

Romans 8:11. But if the Spirit of him that raised up Jesus from the dead dwell in you, he that raised up Christ from the dead shall also quicken your mortal bodies by his Spirit that dwelleth in you.

So there is coming a time for your body to experience the adoption, to wit, the redemption of the body. He does not say that he will give you a new body. Do not believe this modern doctrine. But he shall quicken your mortal body; that is to say, the same body, which is now subject to death, and so is mortal, is to be quickened at the resurrection.

Romans 8:12. Therefore, brethren, we are debtors, not to the flesh, to live after the flesh

What do we owe the old nature? Nothing, surely. Give it a decent burial. Let it be buried with Christ in baptism. Let the Spirit of God come and renew it. But we owe it nothing, and we are not debtors to it.

Romans 8:13-14. For if ye live after the flesh, ye shall die: but if ye through the Spirit do mortify the deeds of the body ye shall live. For as many as are led by the Spirit of God, they are the sons of God.

Your "universal fatherhood" is rubbish. "As many as are led by the Spirit of God, they are the sons of God," and none others. This is the essential to sonship — that we should have the Spirit of God within us.

Romans 8:15-16. For ye have not received the spirit of bondage again to fear: but ye have received the Spirit of adoption, whereby we cry, Abba, Father. The Spirit itself beareth witness with our spirit, that we are the children of God:

That is, when we have the Spirit, when we are renewed in the Spirit of our minds, when we come into the domain of Spirit, and quit the tyranny of the flesh. Then the Spirit beareth witness with our spirit that we are the children of God.

Romans 8:17. And if children, then heirs;

It is not, of course, so in human families. All children are not heirs; but it is so in the family of God.

Romans 8:17. Heirs of God,

What a heritage! God himself becomes our heritage. We are heirs to all that God has, and all that God is.

Romans 8:17. And joint-heirs with Christ; if so be that we suffer with him, that we may be also glorified together.

The whole chapter is rather too long for our reading, so we will pass on to the 28th verse.

Romans 8:28. And we know

This is not a matter of opinion. This is scarcely a matter of faith. "We know." We are sure of it. We have proved it.

Romans 8:28. That all things work together for good to them that love God,

They all work. They work in harmony. They work for one purpose. That purpose is for good.

Romans 8:28. To them who are the called according to his purpose.

That is their private character, which God knows, and which he reveals to them in course of time.

Romans 8:29. For whom he did foreknow, he also did predestinate to be conformed to the image of his Son, that he might be the first-born among many brethren.

This is their character, which they perceive, which others may in a measure perceive. We are to be like him then, conformed to his image; and if we be joint-heirs with him, what a joy it is that we are to be partakers of his nature, made like to him! Christ will be reflected, and in a measure repeated, in all his people; and this shall be the very glory of heaven, that, look which way you will, you shall see either Christ himself or his likeness in his people. If you have ever stood in a room that was full of mirrors everywhere, how wonderfully your own likeness has been repeated! And heaven shall be a mirror chamber, wherein Christ shall be seen in every one of his people. He did predestinate them to be conformed to the image of his Son.

Romans 8:30. Moreover whom he did predestinate, them he also called: and whom he called, them he also justified: and whom he justified, them he also glorified?

That glorification we cannot see as yet. It is in the excessive brightness of the future, just as his divine election is in the brightness of the past. These are the two columns on either shore; but the swinging bridge in between is this — calling and justification. These are joined in one, stud if thou hast either of these, thou mayest know thy predestination and thy future glorification

Romans 8:31. What shall we then say to these things?

Oh! have you not often said that? When you have studied the plan of grace, the covenant of God, have you not said to yourself, "What can I say to all this? It is passing wonder; It exceeds the power of comprehension, for the greatness of this glory. What shall we then say to these things?" Well, we will say something practical that shall cheer our hearts.

Romans 8:31-33. If God be for us who can be against us? He that spared not his own Son, but delivered him up for us all, how shall he not with him also freely give us all things? Who shall lay anything to the charge of God's elect? It is God that justifieth.

It may be read, "God that justifieth?" and properly may be read as a question.

Romans 8:34. Who is he that condemneth? It is Christ that died,

He is the Judge. Will he who died condemn?

Romans 8:34. Yea rather, that is risen again, who is even at the right hand of God, who also maketh intercession for us.

He alone is Judge. Has he done all this, and will he condemn us?

Romans 8:35. Who shall separate us from the love of Christ? shall tribulation, or distress, or persecution, or famine, or nakedness, or peril, or sword?

These have been tried on the saints for ages.

Romans 8:36. As it is written, For thy sake we are killed all the day long: we are accounted as sheep for the slaughter.

But has this divided them from Christ? Hear them all, as with united voice they answer.

Romans 8:37-38. Nay, in all these things we are more than conquerors through him that loved us. For I am persuaded,

Somebody asked, "Pray, what persuasion may you be?" Well, this is my persuasion.

Romans 8:38. That neither death, nor life, nor angels,

Good or bad.

Romans 8:38. Nor principalities, nor powers, nor things present,

Hard and grinding as they may be.

Romans 8:38. Nor things to come.

Unknown mysteries dreaded.

Romans 8:39. Nor height, nor depth, nor any other creature, shall be able to separate us from the love of God, which is in Christ Jesus our Lord.

Verses 14-17

Romans 8:14. For as many as are led by the Spirit of God, they are the sons of God.

You can judge yourself, dear friend, by this test. Do you follow the Spirit's leading? Do you desire continually that he should be your supreme Guide and Leader? If you are led by the Spirit of God, then you have this highest of all privileges, you are one of the sons of God. Nothing can equal that honour; to be a son of God, is more than anything of which ungodly kings and emperors can boast, with all their array of pomp and wealth.

Romans 8:15. For ye have not received the spirit of bondage again to fear;

Ye did receive it once, and it was a great blessing to you. This came of the law, and the law brought you under bondage through a sense of sin, and that made you first cry for liberty, and then made you accept the liberating Saviour; but you have not received that spirit of bondage again to fear.

Romans 8:15. But ye have received the spirit of adoption, whereby we cry, Abba, Father.

We who believe in Jesus are all children of God, and we dare to use that name which only children might use, "Abba;" and we dare use it even in the presence of God, and to say to him, "Abba, Father." We cannot help doing it, because the spirit of adoption must have its own mode of speech; and its chosen way of speaking is to appeal to the great God by this name, "Abba, Father."

Romans 8:16. The Spirit itself beareth witness with our spirit, that we are the children of God:

There are two witnesses, then, and in the mouth of these two witnesses the whole truth about our adoption shall be established. Our own spirit — so changed as to be reconciled to God, and led in ways which once it never trod, — our own spirit bears witness that we are the sons of God; and then God's own Spirit bears witness, too, and so we become doubly sure.

Romans 8:17. And if children, then heirs;

For all God's children are heirs, and all equally heirs. The elder-born members of God's family, such as Abraham and the rest of the patriarchs, are no more heirs of God than are we of these latter days who have but lately come to Christ. "If children, then heirs." Heirs of what?

Romans 8:17. Heirs of God,

Not only heirs of what God chooses to give, but heirs of himself. There need be nothing else said, if this is true: "The Lord is my portion, saith my soul." "Heirs of God,"

Romans 8:17. And joint-heirs with Christ; if so be that we suffer with him, that we may be also glorified together.

Do you ever have in your heart a longing to behold the glory of God? Do you feel pressed down when you see abounding sin? Are your eyes ready to be flooded with tears at the thought of the destruction of the ungodly? Then, you are having sympathy with Christ in his sufferings, and you shall as certainly be an heir with him, by-and-by, in his glory.

This exposition consisted of readings from Psalms 27 and Romans 8:14-17.

Verses 14-30

Romans 8:14. For as many as are led by the Spirit of God, they are the sons of God.

Not those who say they are "the sons of God," but those who undoubtedly prove that they are, by being led, influenced, gently guided, by the Spirit of God.

Romans 8:15. For ye have yet received the spirit of bondage again to fear: but ye have received the Spirit of adoption, whereby we cry, Abba, Father.

We did receive the spirit of bondage once. We felt that we were under the law, and that the law cursed us. We felt its rigorous taxation, and that we could not meet it. Now that spirit 'has gone, and we have the spirit of freedom, the spirit of children, the spirit of adoption. I suppose that the apostle, when he thus spake and said. "ye," felt so much of the spirit of adoption in his own bosom that he could not talk of it as belonging to others alone. He was obliged to include it thus', and so he puts it, "Ye have received the spirit of adoption whereby we cry, Abba, Father." He wanted to intimate that he himself also was a partaker of this blessed spirit. And woe to the preacher who can preach an adoption which he never enjoyed. Woe to any of us if we can teach to others concerning the spirit of sonship, but never feel it crying in our own souls, "Abba, Father."

Romans 8:16. The Spirit itself beareth witness with our spirit, that toe are the children of God:

It corroborates the testimony of conscience. We feel that we are the children of God; and the Spirit of God comes forward as a second, but still greater and higher witness, to confirm the testimony that we are the children of God.

Romans 8:17. And if children then heirs; heirs of God, and joint heirs with Christ; if so be that we suffer with him, that we may be also glorified together.

It is to be all with him. With him in the suffering; with him in the glory; with him in the reproach of men; with him in the honour at the right hand of the Father. But if we shun the path of humiliation with him, we may expect that he will deny us in the day of his glory.

Romans 8:18. For I reckon

Judge, count it up, and calculate.

Romans 8:18. That the sufferings of this present time are not worthy to be compared with the glory which shall be revealed in us.

These sufferings, however sharp, are short, compared with eternal glory, infinitesimal, not worthy to be taken account of; like one drop falling into a river and lost in it.

Romans 8:19-21. For the earnest expectation of the creature waiteth for the manifestation of the sons of God. For the creature was made subject to vanity, not willingly, but by reason of him who hath subjected the same in hope. Because the creature itself also shall be delivered from the bondage of corruption into the glorious liberty of the children of God.

There is a future even for materialism. That poor, dusky clod in which we dwell is yet to be illuminated with the light of God; and these poor bodies which are akin to the dust of the earth, and still remain as if they were not delivered, being subjected to pain, and weakness, and death — even they are yet to be brought into the glorious liberty of the children of God.

Romans 8:22-23. For we know that the whole creation groaneth and travaileth in pain together until now. And not only they, but ourselves also, which have the first fruits of the Spirit, even we ourselves groan within ourselves, waiting for the adoption, to wit, the redemption of our body.

The soul has obtained its redemption. Therefore, our heart is glad, and our glory rejoicing. But our body has not yet obtained its redemption. That is to come at the resurrection. Then will be the adoption. "Waiting for the adoption, to wit, the redemption of our body." Oh! blessed fact! Though now, in common with the whole creation, the body is subjected to bondages, yet it shall be delivered, and we — the whole man, body as well as soul and spirit — shall be brought into the liberty of the children of God.

Romans 8:24-25. For we are saved by hope: but hope that is seen is not hope: for what a man seeth, why doth he yet hope for? But if we hope for that we see not, then do we with patience wait for it.

Ah! brethren, if we could be all we should like to be, there would then be no room for the exercise of hope. If we had all that we are to have, then hope, which is one of the sweetest of the graces, would have no room in which to exercise herself. It is a blessed thing to have hope. Though I have heard that faith and hope are not to be found in heaven, I very much question it. I do not think they will ever die. "Now abide these three —faith, hope, and love"; for in heaven there will be room, surely, for trust in the ever blessed God that he will never cast us out from our blessedness —room for the expectation of the second advent — room for the expectation of the conquest of the world — room for the fulfilled promise of bringing all the elect to glory; still something to be hoped for; still something to be believed. Yet here is the main sphere of hope, and therefore let us give it full scope; and when other graces seem to be at a non-plus, let us still hope. I believe the New Zealand word for hope is "swimming thought," because that will swim when everything else is drowned. Oh! happy is that man who has a hope that swims on the crest of the stormiest billow.

Romans 8:26. Likewise the Spirit also helpeth our infirmities:

And especially our infirmities in prayer, for there is where infirmities are mostly seen.

Romans 8:26. For we knew not what we should pray for as we ought: but the Spirit itself maketh intercession for us with groanings which cannot be uttered.

I should have thought that it would have read, "But the Spirit itself teaches us what we should pray for." But it does more than that. He goes beyond teaching us what we should pray for. He "maketh intercession for us, with groanings which cannot be uttered." Do you know what those groanings are? I am afraid that those who never had groanings which cannot be uttered will never know anything of that glory which cannot be expressed, for that is the way to it. The groanings that cannot be uttered lead on to unutterable joy.

Romans 8:27. And he that searcheth the hearts knoweth what is the mind of the Spirit, because he maketh intercession for the saints according to the will of God.

That is the philosophy of prayer. Whatever God's will is, the Spirit of God writes it on the hearts of praying saints, and they pray for the very thing which God intends to give. As the barometer often foretells the weather that is coming, so the spirit of prayer in the Christian is the barometer which indicates when showers of blessing are coming. It is well with us when we can pray. If we cannot do anything else, if we feel that we can pray, times are not so bad with us as we might think.

Romans 8:28. And we know that all things work together for good to them that love God, to them who are the called according to his purpose.

We know it: we are assured of it.

Romans 8:29-30. For whom he did foreknow, he also did predestinate to be conformed to the image of his Son, that he might be the firstborn among many brethren. Moreover whom he did predestinate, them he also called: and whom he called, them he also justified: and whom he justified, them he also glorified.

No breaking of these links. Where God gives one of these blessings, he gives the rest. There is no intimation of a failure somewhere in between. The predestinated are called, and the called are justified, and the justified are glorified.

Romans 8:31-33. What shall we then say to these things? If God be for us, who can be against us? He that spared not his own Son, but delivered him up for us all, how shall he not with him also freely give us all things? Who shall lay anything to the charge of God's elect?

Who shall? Who may? Who dares?

Romans 8:33-35. It is God that justifieth. Who is he that condemneth? It is Christ that died, yea rather, that is risen again, who is even at the right hand of God, who also maketh intercession for us. Who shall separate us from the love of Christ? shall tribulation, or distress, or persecution, or famine, or nakedness, or peril, or sword?

All these have done their worst.

Romans 8:36. As it is written, For thy sake we are killed all the day long; we are accounted as sheep for the slaughter.

But have they divided the saints from the love of Christ? Have they made the saints leave off loving Christ, or Christ cease from loving his people?

Romans 8:37-39. Way, in all these things we are more than conquerors through him that loved us. For I am persuaded that neither death, nor life, nor angels, nor principalities, nor powers, nor things present, nor things to come. Nor height nor depth, nor any other creature, shall be able to separate us from the love of God, which is in Christ Jesus our Lord.

For which blessed be the name of the adorable Trinity, world without end!

Verses 14-39

Romans 8:14. For as many as are led by the Spirit of God, they are the sons of God.

Leading implies following; and those who are enabled to follow the guidance of the Divine Spirit are most assuredly children of God, for the Lord ever leads his own children. If, then, you are following the lead of God's Spirit, you have one of the evidences of sonship.

Romans 8:15. For ye have not received the spirit of bondage again to fear; but ye have received the Spirit of adoption, whereby we cry, Abba, Father.

The spirit of bondage is the spirit of servants, not of sons; but that servitude is ended for us who are made free in Christ Jesus. We are no longer afraid of being called the children of God. We are not afraid of our own Father; we have a filial fear of him, but it is so mixed with love that there is no torment in it. Whether Jew or Gentile, we cry, "Abba, Father."

Romans 8:16. The Spirit itself beareth witness with our spirit, that we are the children of God:

Our spirit knows that we are God's children and then God's Spirit adds his testimony to the witness of our spirit that we are the children of God.

Romans 8:17. And if children, then heirs; heirs of God, and joint-heirs with Christ; if so be that we suffer with him, that we may be also glorified together.

This would not necessarily be true of any man's family, for he might have children who were not his heirs; but, in God's family, all who are born into it are born "heirs of God, and joint-heirs with Christ." We must take our part of Christ's portion,— his portion here, and his portion hereafter; the rule for us who are in him shall be, "share and share alike." He himself has said, "Where I am, there shall also my servant be;"

151

and all that he has he will divide with us. Are you willing, dear brother, to take shares with Christ? If not, then I question whether you can be rightly reckoned among his saints.

Romans 8:18. For I reckon that the sufferings of this present time are not worthy to be compared with the glory which shall be revealed in us.

"Light afflictions" are contrasted with "an exceeding weight of glory." Temporary afflictions, but for a moment, are to be followed by everlasting crowns that fade not away. What a contrast!

Romans 8:19. For the earnest expectation of the creature waiteth for the manifestation of the sons of God.

All creation is, as it were, watching and waiting on tip-toe for the day when God shall manifest his sons who are at present hidden. In due time, they shall come forth, acknowledged of God, and then shall the whole creation rejoice.

Romans 8:20-23. For the creature was made subject to vanity, not willingly, but by reason of him who hath subjected the same in hope, Because the creature itself also shall be delivered from the bondage of corruption into the glorious liberty of the children of God. For we know that the whole creation groaneth and travaileth in pain together until now. And not only they, but ourselves also, which have the firstfruits of the Spirit, even we ourselves groan within ourselves, waiting for the adoption, to wit, the redemption of our body.

We have already obtained salvation for our souls, but our body is still under bondage,— subject to weariness,— to pain,— to infirmity,— to death; but, by-and-by, with the new creation, our newly-moulded bodies shall be fit to live in the new world, and fit for our newborn souls to inhabit. This is the full redemption for which we are waiting.

Romans 8:24-28. For we are saved by hope: but hope that is seen is not hope: for what a man seeth, why doth he yet hope for? But if we hope for that we see not, then do we with patience wait for it. Likewise the Spirit also helpeth our infirmities: for we know not what we should pray for as we ought: but the Spirit itself maketh intercession for us with groanings which cannot be uttered.. And he that searcheth the hearts knoweth what is the mind of the Spirit, because he maketh intercession for the saints according to the will of God. And we know that all things work together for good to them that love God, to them who are the called according to his purpose.

"We know that all things work together for good." That is a wonderfully positive statement, Paul. There are certain persons, nowadays, who say that we know nothing; yet the apostles constantly say, "We know this," and "We know that." These people tell us that there is a great distinction between believing and knowing,— but, evidently, it is a distinction of which the inspired apostles knew nothing at all. Read the Epistles of John, and note how he continually says, "We know, we know, we know," and how frequently he adds, "We believe," as though believing and knowing were the same thing. Agnostics may declare that they know nothing, if they please; but, as for us who do know, because we believe what we are taught of God in this Book, we will speak. He who has something to say has a right to say it; we know, and therefore we speak. Mark, brethren, how the apostle speaks here; he does not say that all things shall work together for good; no, but that they do work together, they are now working for your present good. This is not merely something which shall eventually turn out right; it is all right now, "We know that all things are working together for good to them that love God, to them who are the called according to his purpose." No sooner does the apostle mention that word "purpose" than he must needs found a long discourse upon it. He was not afraid or ashamed to speak of the purposes of God. There are some preachers who say nothing about God's purpose, or God's decree; they seem to be afraid of it, they say it is "Calvinistic doctrine." Why, it was here, in the Scriptures, long before Calvin was born, so what right have they to call it by his name? Listen to what the apostle has to say:

Romans 8:29-30. For whom he did foreknow, he also did predestinate to be conformed, to the image of his Son, that he might be the firstborn among many brethren. Moreover whom he did predestinate, them he also called: and whom he called, them he also justified: and whom he justified, them he also glorified.

There is no separating these golden links of love and mercy. That foreknowledge, to which all things future are open and present, begins the deed of love. Predestination comes in, and chooses a people for God who shall be eternally his. Upon this, in due time, follows effectual calling, by which the chosen ones are brought out, from the impure mass of mankind, and set apart unto God. Then follows justification by faith, through the precious blood and righteousness of Jesus Christ; and where this is, glory will certainly come, for "whom he justified, them he also glorified."

Romans 8:31-32. What shall we then say to these things? If God be for us, who can be against us? He that spared not his own Son, but delivered him up for us all, how shall he not with him also freely give us all things ?

Notice, it is not simply "freely give us all things;" but, "with him also freely give us all things." You shall get all things with Christ; but you shall get nothing without Christ, for all the other gifts come in this one. God first gave us his Son; and he gives us everything in him.

Romans 8:33. Who shall lay any thing to the charge of God's elect? It is God that justifieth.

Ring out the challenge in heaven itself; trumpet it through all the caverns of hell; let the whole universe hear it: "Who shall lay any thing to the charge of God's elect ?" None can, for "it is God that justifieth," and his justification blocks every charge that is brought against his people.

Who shall the Lord's elect condemn?
'Tis God that justifies their souls;

And mercy like a mighty stream,
O'er all their sins divinely rolls.

Romans 8:34. Who is he that condemneth ?

None will answer to that challenge, for

Romans 8:34-35. It is Christ that died, yea rather, that is risen again, who is even at the right hand of God, who also maketh intercession for us. Who shall separate us from the love of Christ ?

Oh, this blessed question — this touching question! It seems to come at the end of all the others,— a rear-guard which effectually prevents our treasures from being taken from us. "Quis separabit?" "Who shall separate us from the love of Christ?"

Romans 8:35. Shall tribulation ?

That has been tried. Have not the saints been beaten like wheat upon the threshing-floor? Has not addiction been to them a stern test of the reality of their faith? But Christ has loved them none the less for all the suffering that he has permitted to fall upon them.

Romans 8:35. Or distress, or persecution, or famine, or nakedness, or peril, or sword?

When they have been in famine or poverty, has Christ ever forsaken his saints? Ah, no! he has loved them all the more. Have any of these things separated us from our Saviour? No; but they have, to our own consciousness, knitted us even more closely to our Divine Lord. Cruel men have tried every form of persecuting the saints of God; they have been more inventive in the torments which they have applied to Christians than in almost anything else; yet no torture, no rack, no imprisonment, has ever divided them from Christ. They have clung to him still, after the manner of John Bunyan, who, when they said, that he might go free if he would promise not to preach the gospel, said, "I will

155

lie in prison till the moss grows on my eyelids rather than I will ever make such a promise as that. If you let me out of prison today, I will preach tomorrow, by the grace of God."

Romans 8:36. As it is written, For thy sake we are killed all the day long; we are accounted as sheep for the slaughter.

But there has been no triumph over the saints in this case.

Romans 8:37-39. Nay, in all these things we are more than conquerors through him that loved us. For I am persuaded, that neither death, nor life, nor angels, nor principalities, nor powers, nor things present, nor things to come, nor height, nor depth, nor any other creature, shall be able to separate us from the love of God, which is in Christ Jesus our Lord.

Not all that men on earth can do,
Nor powers on high, nor powers below,
Shall cause his mercy to remove,
Or wean our hearts from Christ our love.
Glory be unto his holy name! Amen.

Verses 15-31

Romans 8:15. For ye have not received the spirit of bondage again to fear;

You did receive it once. You needed it. You were in sin, and it was well for you when sin became bondage to you. It was grievous, but it was salutary; but you have not received the spirit of bondage again to fear.

Romans 8:15. But ye have received the Spirit of adoption, whereby we cry, Abba, Father.

Does your spirit cry in that way tonight? Even if you be in the dark, yet if you cry for your Father, you will soon be in the light. There is no need to be distressed with any form of doubt so long as the Spirit makes this continual breathing, "Abba, Father, show thyself to me. Do what thou wilt to me. Let me taste thy love. Let me at least bow under thy hand."

Romans 8:16. The Spirit itself beareth witness with our spirit, that we are the children of God.

Our spirit feels the spirit of adoption, and so there is a double witness, the witness of our spirit, and the witness of God's Spirit, that we are the children of God. In the mouth of these two witnesses the whole shall be established.

Romans 8:17. And if children, then heirs;

That does not follow in other cases, but it does in the case of the family of God. In a man's family, only one son can be an heir; but in God's family, of all is it declared "if children, then heirs."

Romans 8:17. Heirs of God,

Not only heirs to God, but heirs of God. God himself is the heritage of his people; he belongs to them now, as an eternal endowment. "Heirs of God."

Romans 8:17. And joint heirs with Christ; if so be that we suffer with him, that we may be also glorified together.

We are to take the rough and the smooth, the bitter and the sweet, with Christ; and who will make any demur to that? If we are to be heirs with Christ, we do not wish to split the inheritance in pieces. Nay! we will take the cross as well as the crown — the reproach as well as the honour.

Romans 8:18. For I reckon that the sufferings of this present time are not worthy to be compared with the glory which shall be revealed in us.

He had just mentioned the sufferings. They are too little. They are mere specks in the sun. They are too small to be weighed in comparison with the exceeding weight of glory which God has prepared for us.

Romans 8:19. For the earnest expectation of the creature waiteth for the manifestly, of the sons of God.

So great is to be the glory of God's children that all the world is waiting for it. Every creature stands on tip-toe, looking for the coming of Christ and the manifestation of the redeemed. What must be the greatness of this thing which the whole creation has learned to expect?

Romans 8:20-21. For the creature was made subject to vanity, not willingly, but by reason of him who hath subjected the same in hope. Because the creature itself also shall be delivered from the bondage of corruption into the glorious liberty of the children of God.

We were in bondage, and we have come out in a measure into the liberty of the children of God. Now the world in which we live is in sympathy with us, and it is part under bondage because of sin, but it is only temporary bondage. There will come a day when the whole creation shall be delivered from the bondage of corruption into the glorious liberty of the children of God — a new heavens and a new earth, wherein dwelleth righteousness.

Romans 8:22. For we know that the whole creation groaneth and travaileth in pain together until now.

Deep groans are in the world. Have you not heard of earthquakes? Do you not know how the whole world is in a tremor? There is something coming, and all the world is groaning for that coming. God makes the universe to be like an instrument of music played upon by the fingers of mortal men: so that when they are sorrowful, the world is sorrowful, and when they go forth with joy and are led forth with peace, then the mountains and the hills shall break forth before them into singing, and all the trees of the field shall clap their hands. "We know that the whole creation groaneth and travaileth in pain together until now."

Romans 8:23. And not only they, but ourselves also, which have the first fruits of the Spirit, even we ourselves groan within ourselves, waiting for the adoption, to wit, the redemption of our body.

As yet the body is under bondage. The body is dead because of sin: hence those headaches — this palpitation of the heart — this heaviness of the day which incases us: but by-and-bye, as the material world is to be delivered from its bondage, so shall these bodies also pass away from all the encumbrance of weakness, and disease, and death, into a better state.

Romans 8:24. Far we are saved by hope:

As yet.

Romans 8:24-25. But hope that is seen is not hope: for what a man seeth, why doth he yet hope for? But if we hope for that we see not, then do we with patience wait for it.

What a lesson that is, and how seldom do we learn it! Oh! in this present state our main duty is, "Then do we with patience wait for it." You want to have your cake and keep it. but you cannot eat it and keep it too. With patience wait for it. There see some fruits of the earth that are not ripe yet. You lay them by in store, and there are many good things that God has laid by in store for his people, and he says to us, "With patience wait for it:" Oh! but you would fain have heavenly joy on earthly ground. It would be a sorry misfit if it were so. But God keeps time and season, and there is harmony in his music. You shall have earthly sorrow on earthly ground, and you shall have heavenly bliss on the heavenly shore: but not till then. We do with patience wait for it.

Romans 8:26. Likewise the Spirit also helpeth our infirmities;

Especially our infirmities in prayer. I think that if anywhere our infirmities come out, it is in prayer: even the strongest are, on their knees, comparatively weak. How few there are among us that prevail with God. as Elias did! We ought to do so. We need, none of us, stop short of the fullest stature of a man in Christ Jesus. and a man of full stature in Christ would surely carry the keys of heaven's treasury at his girdle. He would have but to ask, and to receive — to seek and to find. May the Spirit help our infirmities.

Romans 8:26. For we know not what we should pray for as we ought: but the Spirit itself maketh intercession for us with groanings which cannot be uttered.

See what little worlds we are. Microcosms, — to use a harder word; for as there are groanings and travailings in the whole creation, so are there such in the little world of our own heart. Only nature's travail is but natural; but our travail is supernatural. It is the Spirit himself groaning within chosen breasts with groanings that cannot be uttered.

Romans 8:27. And he that searcheth the hearts knoweth what is the mind of the Spirit, because he maketh intercession for the saints according to the will of God.

When we ourselves hardly know the mind of the Spirit, he that searches all hearts knows it. When we feel as if we could not pray, yet the Spirit of God makes intercession in us, and the great Father reads the purport of the intercessions, and blesses us, not according to our knowledge of our own prayer, but according to his knowledge of what the Spirit means by those prayers. Have you never noticed that holy men of old sometimes spoke much greater things than they thought they should, for the Spirit of God in them spoke by them more than they themselves understood; and I believe that it is so in prayer. Oh! oftentimes the groaning, wrestling believer may have no inkling of the full purport of his own prayer, but he that searcheth the hearts knoweth what is the mind of the Spirit, because he maketh intercession for the saints according to the will of God.

Romans 8:28. And we know –

Now we are getting upon a dear old passage which reads like music. There is no eloquence in the world that ever touches the eloquence of the Apostle here.

Romans 8:28. That all things work together for good to them that love God, to them who are the called according to his purpose.

I do not like to hear this text quoted, as I often do, only in part — only half of it. "All things work together for good," say people. "Oh! yes; somehow or other, good will come of it." It does not say so here. It says, "All things work together for good to them that love God; to them that are the called according to his purpose." A special purpose and object of God for a special people. And if you do not belong to this people, things are not working together for your good. No; but you may find that they will work together for your banishment from life and from the presence of God. Take your heed to this. The stars in their courses fight against you, if you fight against God; and the very earth groans and complains of bearing up your weight if you are a rebel against the Most High. You must, first of all, be reconciled so as to love God, and the eternal purpose must be wrought in you by your effectual calling from out of the world, or else you must not dare to intrude into the holy sanctuary of my text. "We know that all things work together for good to them that love God." Of course, they do, for God loves them. "To them that are the called according to his purpose." Of course, they do, for that purpose which called them is not consistent with anything, but a purpose of infinite love to them. The great eternal purpose encompasses all things that happen, and bends all to the grand object of the good of the called ones.

Romans 8:29-30. For whom he did foreknow, he also did predestinate to be conformed to the image of his Son, that he might be the firstborn among many brethren. Moreover whom he did predestinate, them he also called: and whom he called, them he also justified: and whom he justified, them he also glorified.

He spoke of it as if it were done because it is so sure, so certain to be done; he puts it down as a fact.

Romans 8:31. What shall we then say to these things?

Ah! indeed, what shall we say? If we had the tongues of men and angels, what could we say? Well, we will say this much at any rate.

Romans 8:31. If God be for us, who can be against us?

Those afflictions that we read of just now — these reproaches which we share with Christ — what of them? They are not worth calling anything. "If God be for us, who can be against us?"

Verses 18-39

Romans 8:18. For I reckon that the sufferings of this present time are not worthy to be compared with the glory which shall be revealed in us.

Paul made "the sufferings of this present time" into a matter of simple arithmetic and careful reckoning. He added them all up, and saw what the total was, he seemed to be about to state a proportion sum, but he gave it up, and said that the sufferings were "not worthy to be compared with the glory which shall be revealed." Did they stand as one to a thousand? No, else they had been worthy to be compared. Did they stand as one to ten thousand, — or one to a million, — or one to a million of millions? If so, they would still have been worthy to be compared; but Paul saw that there was no proportion whatever between them. The sufferings seemed to be but as a single drop, and the glory to be as a boundless ocean.

"Not worthy to be compared with the glory which shall be revealed in us."

That glory is not yet fully revealed; it is revealed to us, but not yet in us. What, then, shall we do in the meantime? Why, wait with patience, and bear our appointed burden until the time comes for us to be relieved of it; — wait, however, with hope, — wait, too, as we must, quietly enduring the pains and pangs which precede so glorious a birth. In this respect, we are not alone, as the apostle goes on to say, —

Romans 8:19-22. For the earnest expectation of the creature waiteth for the manifestation of the sons of God. For the creature was made subject to vanity, not willingly, but by reason of him who hath subjected the same in hope, Because the creature itself also shall be delivered from the bondage of corruption into the glorious liberty of the children of God. For we know that the whole creation groaneth and travaileth in pain together until now.

We live in a world that is under a curse, — a world that was made subject to bondage through human sin. What means this cold? What mean these fogs? What mean the general mourning and sighing of the air all through the winter? What mean the disturbances, and convulsions, and catastrophes that we hear about on all hands? It is the creation groaning, travailing, waiting, — waiting till there shall be a new heaven and a new earth, because the former things shall have passed away.

Romans 8:23. And not only they, but ourselves also, which have the firstfruits of the spirit, even we ourselves groan within ourselves, waiting for the adoption, to wit, the redemption of our body.

Our soul has been delivered from the curse. The redemption of the soul is complete, but not yet that of the body. That must suffer pain and weariness, and even descend into the tomb, but its day of manifestation shall surely come. At the appearing of our Lord from heaven, then shall the body itself be delivered, and the whole creation shall also be delivered, so we wait in a travailing condition; and we may well be content to wait, for these pangs within us and around all signify the glorious birth for which we may wait in hope.

Romans 8:24-25. For we are saved by hope: but hope that is seen is not hope: for what a man seeth, why doth he yet hope for? But if we hope for that we see not, then do we with patience wait for it.

This is our attitude and our condition now, — waiting for the glory which is to be revealed in us, and accepting the sorrow which is appointed to us as an introduction to the joy which is to come to us mysteriously, through it but while we are waiting, we are not without present comfort.

Romans 8:26. Likewise the Spirit also helpeth our infirmities: for we know not what we should pray for as we ought: but the Spirit itself maketh intercession for us with groanings which cannot be uttered.

You must, I am sure, as children of God, often have felt that Spirit within you groaning in prayer what you could not express. How often have you risen from your knees feeling the utter inadequacy of words to express the desires of your heart! And you have felt that you had larger desires than you have been able to interpret. There have been mighty pangs within you telling of the presence of this wrestling spirit.

Romans 8:27. And he that searcheth the hearts knoweth what is the mind of the Spirit,

When you do not know your own mind, God knows the mind of the Spirit, and that is the very essence of prayer. He "knoweth what is the mind of the Spirit," —

Romans 8:27. Because he maketh intercession for (or, in) the saints according to the will of God.

Whatever the spirit of God prompts us to pray for, is according to the mind of God, for it is not possible that the Holy Spirit should ever be otherwise than in perfect accord with the Divine Father. The eternal degrees, if we could read them, would convey to us the same truth as the impulses of the Spirit in our heart. And this is the true exploration of prayer, — that what God intends to do, his spirit leads his people to ask him to do; and thus there is no conflict between the eternal predestination of God and the earnest entreaties of his people. They are, in fact, the outcome of that very predestination.

Romans 8:28-30. And we know that all things work together for good to them that love God, to them who are the called according to his purpose. For whom he did foreknow, he also did predestinate to be conformed to the image of his Son, that he might be the firstborn among many brethren. Moreover whom he did predestinate, them he also called: and whom he called, them he also justified: and whom he justified, them he also glorified.

These great truths must never be separated. Any one of these things befog true of us, it is most certain that the rest are also true. Now, my dear brother, you cannot read God's foreknowledge, neither can you enter into the secrets of predestination; but you can tell whether you are called, or not; you can know whether you are justified by faith, or not;

and if you get hold of those links, you have got a grip of that endless chain which is firmly fastened to the granite rock of eternity past, and which is also fastened to the rock of the glorious eternity which is yet to be revealed.

Romans 8:31-33. What shall we then say to these things? If God be for us, who can be against us? He that spared not his own Son, but delivered him up for us all, how shall he not with him also freely give us all things? Who shall lay any thing to the charge of God's elect? It is God that justifieth.

For so we think it ought to be read. That is another question. Can God lay anything to our charge after having justified us? Will he contradict himself?

Romans 8:34. Who is he that condemneth?

There is only One who can, for there is only one Judge, and that Judge is Jesus. So, the apostle puts it again in the form of a question, — shall he condemn us?

Romans 8:34. It is Christ that died, yea rather, that is risen again, who is even at the right hand of God, who also maketh intercession for us.

Shall he condemn us? It is altogether impossible.

Romans 8:35. Who shall separate us from the love of Christ? shall tribulation, or distress, or persecution, or famine, or nakedness, or peril, or sword ?

What a long list of ills! They seem to make up a Jeremiah's roll of sorrow. Can they separate us from the love of Christ? They have all been tried; have they ever succeeded?

Romans 8:36. As it is written, For thy sake we are killed all the day long; we are accounted as sheep for the slaughter.

But did they succeed in separating saints from the love of Christ even in the days of martyrdom?

Romans 8:37-39. Nay, in all these things we are more than conquerors through him that loved us. For I am persuaded, that neither death, nor life, nor angels, nor principalities, nor powers, nor things present, nor things to come, nor height, nor depth, nor any other creature, shall be able to separate us from the love of God, which is in Christ Jesus our Lord.

"Wherefore, comfort one another with these words."

Verses 19-39

Romans 8:19. For the earnest expectation of the creature waiteth for the manifestation of the sons of God.

The whole creation is in a waiting posture, waiting for the glory yet to be revealed.

Romans 8:20-21. For the creature was made subject to vanity, not willingly, but by reason of him who hath subjected the same in hope, Because the creature itself also shall be delivered from the bondage of corruption into the glorious liberty of the children of God.

Everything here is blighted, and subject to storm, or to decay, or to sudden death, or to calamity of some sort. It is a fair world, but there is the shadow of the curse over it all. The slime of the serpent is on all our Edens now. "The creature itself was made subject to vanity," but it "also shall be delivered from the bondage of corruption into the glorious liberty of the children of God."

Romans 8:22. For we know that the whole creation groaneth and travaileth in pain together until now.

The birth-pangs of the creation are on it; the living creature within is moving itself to break its shell, and come forth.

Romans 8:23. And not only they, but ourselves also, which have the first fruits of the Spirit, even we ourselves groan within ourselves, waiting for the adoption, to wit, the redemption of our body.

That is our state now; at least, it is the condition of the most of us. Some of our brethren have gone ahead so tremendously that they have passed out of the world of groaning altogether; they are perfect. I regret that they are not in heaven; it would seem to be a much more proper place for them than this imperfect earth is. But as for us, our experience leads us, in sympathy with the apostle, to say that we are groaning after something better. We have not received it yet; we have the beginnings of it, we have the earnest of it, we have the sure pledge of it; but it is not as yet our portion to enjoy; we are "waiting for the adoption, to wit, the redemption of our body;" for, though the soul be born again, the body is not. "The body in dead," says the apostle, in the tenth verse of this chapter, "because of sin; but the spirit is life because of righteousness." There is a wonderful process through which this body shall yet pass, and then it shall be raised again, a glorious body, fitted for our regenerated spirit; but as yet it remains unregenerate.

Romans 8:24. For we are saved by hope:

Hope contains the major part of our salvation within itself.

Romans 8:24-26. But hope that is seen is not hope: for what a man seeth, why doth he yet hope for? But if we hope for that we see not, then do we with patience wait for it. Likewise the Spirit also helpeth our infirmities:

That same Spirit who gave us the spirit of adoption, that same Spirit who set us longing for something higher and better, "also helpeth our infirmities;" and we have so many of them that we show them even when we are on our knees.

Romans 8:26. For we know not what we should pray for as we ought: but the Spirit himself maketh intercession for us with groanings which cannot be uttered.

There seems to be a good deal of this groaning; it is only in heaven that there are- "No groans to mingle with the songs which warble from immortal tongues." But down here a groan is sometimes the fittest wheel for the chariot of progress. We sigh, and cry, and groan, to grow out of ourselves, and to grow more like our Lord, and so to become more fit for the glory which shall be revealed in us.

Romans 8:27. And he that searcheth the hearts knoweth what is the mind of the Spirit, because he maketh intercession for the saints according to the will of God.

That is the whole process of prayer. The Spirit of God knows the will of the Father, and he comes and writes it on our hearts. A true prayer is the revelation of the Spirit of God to our heart, making us desire what God has appointed to give to us. Hence the success of prayer is no difficulty to the predestinarian. Some foolishly say, "If God has ordained everything, what is the use of praying?" If God had not ordained everything, there would be no use in praying; but prayer is the shadow of the coming mercy which falls across the spirit, and we become in prayer in some degree gifted like the seers of old. The spirit of prophecy is upon the man who knows how to pray; the Spirit of God has moved him to ask for what God is about to give.

Romans 8:28. And we know that all things work together for good to them that love God,

"All things." That is a very comprehensive expression, is it not? It includes your present trouble, your aching head, your heavy heart: "all things." "All things work." There is nothing idle in God's domain. "All things work together." There is no discord in the providence of God. The strangest ingredients go to make up the one matchless medicine for all our maladies. "All things work together for good" — for lasting and eternal good, — "to them that love God," that is their outward character, —

Romans 8:28. To them who are the called according to his purpose.

That is their secret character, and the reason why they love God at all.

Romans 8:29. For whom he did foreknow, he also did predestinate to be conformed to the image of his Son, that he might be the firstborn among many brethren.

Oh, what a glorious privilege is yours and mine, if we are indeed children of God! We are, in some respects, children of God in the same sense as Christ himself is; he is the firstborn, and we are among his "many brethren."

Romans 8:30. Moreover whom he did predestinate, them he also called: and whom he called, them he also justified: and whom he justified, them he also glorified.

Notice that personal pronoun "he" — how it comes at the beginning, and goes on to the end. "Salvation is of the Lord." This is so often forgotten that, trite as it may appear, we cannot repeat it too often: "Whom he did foreknow, he also did predestinate whom he did predestinate, them he also called, and whom he called, them he also justified: and whom he justified, them he also glorified." You might suppose, from the talk of some men, that, salvation is all of the man himself; — that is free agency pushed into a falsehood, a plain truth puffed into a lie. There is such a thing as free agency, and we should make a great mistake if we forgot it; but there is also such a thing as free grace, and we shall make a still greater mistake if we limit that to the agency of man; it is God who works our salvation from the beginning to the end.

Romans 8:31. What shall we then say to these things? If God be for us, who can be against us?

If God is that great working One who does all this, who can be against us? "Why, a great many," says one. But they are nothing, nor are all put together anything at all, as compared with him who is on our side.

Romans 8:32-33. He that spared not his own Son, but delivered him up for us all, how shall he not with him also freely give us all things? Who shall lay anything to the charge of God's elect? It is God that justifieth?

No, that is impossible; and if he does not lay anything to their charge, what cause have they to fear?

Spurgeon's Verse Exposition On Romans

Romans 8:34. Who is he that condemneth? It is Christ that died.

What, die for them, and then condemn them? Nobody can condemn them but the Judge; and if he is unable to condemn them, in consequence of what he has already done for them, then none can. But this is not all.

Romans 8:34. Yea rather, that is risen again, who is even at the right hand of God, who also maketh intercession for us.

Will he blow hot and mild, and first intercede for them, and then condemn them? It cannot be.

Romans 8:35. Who shall separate us from the love of Christ?

"Quis separabit?" That shall be our motto in every time of trial: "who shall separate us from the love of Christ?"

Romans 8:35-36. Shall tribulation, or distress, or persecution, or famine, or nakedness, or peril, or sword, As it is written, For thy sake we are killed all the day long; we are accounted as sheep for the slaughter.

They have all had their turn; but did any of them, or all of them put together, ever divide the saints from Christ?

Romans 8:37-39. Nay, in all these things we are more than conquerors through him that loved us. For I am persuaded, that neither death, nor life, nor angels, nor principalities, nor powers, nor things present, nor things to come, nor height, nor depth, nor any other creature, shall be able to separate us from the love of God, which is in Christ Jesus our Lord.

Blessed, forever blessed, be his holy name! Amen.

172

Verses 23-39

Romans 8:23. And not only they, but ourselves also, which have the firstfruits of the Spirit, even we ourselves groan within ourselves, waiting for the adoption, to wit, the redemption of our body.

That is what we are waiting for: " the redemption of our body; " and we shall not wait in vain for it, for Christ is the Saviour of our body as well as of our soul, and the day shall come when even our bodies shall be free from pain, and weakness, and weariness, and sin, and death. Happy day! we may well look forward to it with the loftiest anticipations.

Romans 8:24-25. For we are saved by hope: but hope that is seen is not hope: for what a man seeth, why doth he yet hope for? But if we hope for that we see not, then do we with patience wait for it?

This is our present position, patiently waiting for "the glorious appearing of the great God and our Saviour Jesus Christ," patiently waiting for "the manifestation of the sons of God," for "it doth not yet appear what we shall be; but we know that, when he shall appear, we shall be like him; for we shall see him as he is."

Romans 8:26. Likewise the Spirit also helpeth our infirmities: for we know not what we should pray for as we ought: but the Spirit itself maketh intercession for us with groanings which cannot be uttered.

There is much in this chapter about groaning, and that is but natural, for it so largely concerns our present imperfect state; but, by-and-by, there will be "No groans to mingle with the songs which warble from immortal tongues."

Romans 8:27. And he that searcheth the hearts knoweth what is the mind of the Spirit, because he maketh intercession for the saints according to the will of God.

This explains what to many is the mystery of prayer. The Holy Spirit, being himself God, knows the secret purposes of the divine will, and therefore moves the saints to pray in accordance with that will, and makes their supplications effectual through his own prevailing intercession.

Romans 8:28. And we know—

Paul, like John, was no agnostic; he did not even say, "We think, we imagine, we suppose." No; " we know"—

Romans 8:28. That all things work together for good—

We must not stop there, otherwise the statement will not be true, for all things do not work together for good to all men, but only—

Romans 8:28. To them that love God, to them who are the called according to his purpose.

How are we to know who they are who are the called according to God's eternal purpose? The previous clause informs us, for both relate to the same individuals; " them that love God" are " them who are the saved according to his purpose." We cannot peer into the pages of the Lamb's book of life, yet we can tell by this simple test whether our names are recorded there, do we truly love the Lord? If so, all things are working for our present and eternal good, all things visible and invisible, all things friendly and unfriendly, all things in providence and grace.

Romans 8:29. For whom he did foreknow, he also did predestinate to be conformed to the image of his Son, that he might be the firstborn among many brethren."

What an eternal honour for all believers, that they might be among the "many brethren" of Christ, God's firstborn and well-beloved Son! Here too, we see the purpose of God's foreknowledge and predestination, that we should be " conformed to the image of his Son."

Romans 8:30. Moreover whom he did predestinate, them he also called: and whom he called, them he also justified: and whom he justified, them he also glorified.

You see that these great declarations relate to the same persons right through the whole series: "Whom he did foreknow, he also did predestinate;... whom he did predestinate, them he also called,... them he also justified,... them he also glorified." There is not a single link missing from the eternal purpose and foreknowledge of God to the everlasting glory in which the saints' bliss shall be consummated. The practical question's for each one of us to answer are just these, have I been "called" by grace out of nature's darkness into God's marvelous light? Have I been "justified" by faith, and have I peace with God through our Lord Jesus Christ? Then, being called and justified, I may rest assured that I have been predestinated, and that in due time I shall be glorified.

"There, where my blessed Jesus reigns,
In heaven's unmeasured space,
I'll spend a long eternity In pleasure and in praise."

Romans 8:31-32. What shall we then say to these things? If God be for us who can be against us? He that spared not his own Son, but delivered him up for us all, how shall he not with him also give us all things.

After having given us his own Son, what is there that he can withhold from us if it is for our real good? Nay, he has already virtually given us all things in giving him to us.

Romans 8:33-34. Who shall lay anything to the charge of God's elect? It is God that justifieth. Who is he that condemneth? It is Christ that died, yea rather, that is risen again, who is even at the right hand of God, who also maketh intercession for us.

Well might the apostle ring out these confident challenges to heaven, and earth, and hell. As it is God that justifieth, who can bring any charge against his elect? Who can condemn those for whom Christ died, for whom he has risen, and for whom he is now making intercession at the right hand of God?

Romans 8:35-37. Who shall separate us from the love of Christ? Shall tribulation, or distress, or persecution, or famine, or nakedness, or peril, or sword? As it is written, for thy sake we are killed all the day long; we are accounted as sheep for the slaughter. Nay, in all these things we are more than conquerors through him that loved us.

"All these things" have only made the saints cling the more closely to their Lord, instead of separating them from him. Their persecutors thought they were triumphing over them, but it was the martyrs who were the victors all the while.

Romans 8:38-39. For I am persuaded, that neither death, nor life, nor angels, nor principalities, nor powers, nor things present, nor things to come, Nor height, nor depth, nor any other creature, shall be able to separate us from the love of God, which is in Christ Jesus our Lord.

Paul had good reason for being persuaded that there was no separation for those for whom there was no condemnation, may we be among them by God's grace! Amen.

Verses 26-30

Romans 8:26. Likewise the Spirit also helpeth our infirmities: for we know not what we should pray for as we ought: but the Spirit itself maketh intercession for us with groanings which cannot be uttered.

Groanings, then, are prayers, and prayers which the Spirit of God most certainly hears. And those desires which altogether exhaust language, or which cannot be put into language by reason of the exhaustion of our sorrow, these are nevertheless heard of God, for the Spirit of God is in them.

Romans 8:27. And he that searcheth the hearts knoweth what is the mind of the Spirit, because he maketh intercession for the saints according to the will of God.

That is, when the mind lies still, and God the Holy Spirit writes his will upon it, and also writes God's will. Hence such prayers are sure to be effectual, for they are but the shadow of God's secret purpose falling upon the soul as a kind of prelude to the coming fulfillment of that purpose. Saints' prayers are prophets of God's mercies. We are sure of it; we have no doubt whatever; we know it by experience, as well as by revelation.

Romans 8:28. And we know that all things work together for good to them that love God,

Not yet "all mankind," but these who "love God."

Romans 8:28. To them who are the called according to his purpose.

For they would never have loved God if he had not called them to it, and had not purposed to call them.

Romans 8:29-30. For whom he did foreknow, he also did predestinate to be conformed to the image of his Son, that he might be the firstborn among many brethren. Moreover whom he did predestinate, them he also called: and whom he called, them he also justified: and whom he justified, them he also glorified.

One is tempted to linger over that golden chain, and examine every link. It will suffice, however, to observe that every link is well fastened to the next. Where there is the "foreknowledge," which is alias the "forelove," there is also "elect" — there must be "called" — there shall certainly be "justification," and where that is, there must be "glory."

This exposition consisted of readings from Romans 8:26-30; Revelation 21:10-27; Revelation 22 :l-5.

Verses 26-39

Romans 8:26. Likewise the Spirit also helpeth our infirmities:

Oh, how many these are! Want of memory, want of faith, want of earnestness, ignorance, pride, deadness, coldness of heart, — these are some of our infirmities; but, thank God, we have the omnipotent Spirit of God to help us.

Romans 8:26. For we know not what we should pray for as we ought: but the Spirit itself maketh intercession for us with groanings which cannot be uttered.

These groanings are too deep, too full of meaning to be expressed in words. There are some things the Christian wants for which he cannot ask; perhaps he does not even know what it is that he wants. There is a vacuum in his heart, but he does not know what would fill it. There is a hunger in his spirit, but he knows not what the bread is, nor where the bread is, that can satisfy his wants. But the Holy Ghost can articulate these unuttered groans, and the deepest needs of our soul can thus be brought before God by his own Spirit. You, then, who find it difficult to pray, do not give up praying. The devil tells you that such poor prayers as yours are can never reach the ear of God. Do not believe him. The Spirit helps your infirmities: and when he helps you, you shall, you must prevail.

Romans 8:27. And he that searcheth the hearts knoweth what is the mind of the Spirit, because he maketh intercession for the saints according to the will of God.

It cannot be supposed that the Father does not know what is the mind of the Spirit, since they are one God, and, moreover, inasmuch as the Spirit of God never intercedes for anything which is not according to God's will, we are sure that our heavenly Father will grant every Spirit-indited prayer.

179

Romans 8:28. And we know that all things work together for good to them that love God, to them who are the called according to his purpose."

Almost everything in this world looks to us to be in confusion, but to God's eye all is in order. One wave dashes this way, and another that, but they are all working together, and they are all working with one great purpose too. Say not, Christian, "All these things are against me." Ah, poor soul! this is the verdict of your unbelief, but you will know better than that one of these days. All things are working for you, and not one of them is working against you; therefore, be not dismayed. They are all working together for good to those who love God, to those who are the called according to his purpose.

Romans 8:29. For whom he did foreknow, he also did predestinate to be conformed to the image of his Son, that he might be the firstborn among many brethren.

That was the very end and object of their predestination that they might become like Christ, their great perfect elder Brother.

"'Christ, be my first elect,' he said,
Then chose our souls in Christ our Head
Before he gave the mountains birth
Or laid foundations for the earth."

Romans 8:30. Moreover whom he did predestinate, them he also called:

My soul, hast thou been called of God? Has the Spirit of God ever called thee? If so, rejoice in thy predestinator. Have no doubts and fears concerning that matter, for he would never have called thee if he had not intended to save thee from before the foundation of the world.

Romans 8:30. And whom he called, them he also justified: and whom he justified, them he also glorified.

180

My son, dost thou believe in Jesus? Hast thou trusted in his precious blood? Then thou art justified. Never give way, then, to any fears concerning thine eternal salvation, for, as surely as there is a heaven, thou shalt be a partaker of its glories, for never was there a soul justified who was not afterwards glorified.

Romans 8:31. What shall we then say to these things? If God be for us, who can be against us?

Hast thou the world against the Christian? What is the opposition of the world when God is on thy side? Is thine own heart against thee? What then? God is greater than thy heart. Is the devil against thee? Ah! he is mighty, but God is almighty, and he shall bruise Satan under your feet shortly. Paul was no fanatic; he was a man of great experience and of sound sense; yet he makes nothing of all our foes when God is on our side.

Romans 8:32. He that spared not his own Son, but delivered him up for us all, how shall he not with him also freely give us all things?

When God gave us Christ, he gave us everything, for all the blessings of this life and of the life that is to come lie hidden in Christ as the kernel is within the shell of the nut. What encouragement we have here for believing prayer! Christian, Christ is the golden key of God's treasuries; you have but to use him aright, and whatever you need shall be yours.

Romans 8:33. Who shall lay any thing to the charge of God's elect?

Here is true boldness; Paul, who called himself the very chief of sinners dares to challenge anyone to lay anything to the charge of God's elect? Surely God can do so. No," says Paul, —

Romans 8:33. It is God that justifieth.

He is both just and the Justifier of all who believe in Jesus, and they are

"God's elect."

Romans 8:34. Who is he that condemneth?

"Why," saith one, "Christ, the great Judge, will condemn." No, that he will not, for —

Romans 8:34. It is Christ that died, yea rather, that is risen again, who is even at the right hand of God, who also maketh intercession for us.

Christian, as Christ makes intercession for you, he will never condemn you. Did he shed his blood for you, and yet will he cast you into hell? Did he rise from the dead for you, and yet will he leave you among the dead and the lost? Think not so strangely of the Christ of God, who is the same yesterday, and today, and forever, and who will never condemn those who trust in him.

Romans 8:35. Who shall separate us from the love of Christ? shall tribulation, or distress, or persecution, or famine, or nakedness, or peril, or sword?

They have been tried again and again.

Romans 8:36. It is written, For thy sake we are killed all the day long; we are accounted as sheep for the slaughter.

What was the effect of this persecution? Were the saints turned away from Christ by it?

Romans 8:37-39. Nay, in all these things, we are more than conquerors through him that loved us. For I am persuaded, that neither death, nor life, nor angels, nor principalities, nor powers, nor things present, nor things to come, nor height, nor depth, nor any other creature, shall be able to separate us from the love of God, which is in Christ Jesus our Lord.

Verses 28-39

Romans 8:28-30. And we know that all things work together for good to them that love God, to them who are the called according to his purpose. For whom he did foreknow, he also did predestinate to be conformed to the image of his Son, that he might be the firstborn among many brethren. Moreover whom he did predestinate, them he also called: and whom he called, them he also justified: and whom he justified, them he also glorified.

No breaks between the links of this chain. Foreknowledge is welded to the predestination: the predestination is infallibly linked with the calling, the calling with the justification, and the justification with the glorification. There is no hint given that there may be a flaw or break in the series. Get a hold of any one, and you possess the whole. The called man is the predestinated man. Let him be sure of that. And the justified man shall be a glorified man. Let him have no doubt whatever about that.

Romans 8:31. What shall we then say to these things? If God be for us, who can be against us?

A great many, but they are all nothing. If God be for us, all they that be against us are not worth mentioning: they are ciphers. If he were on their side, then the one would swell the ciphers to the full, but if he be not there, we may put them all into the scale and reckon them as less than nothing.

Romans 8:32-33. He that spared not his own Son, but delivered him up for us all, how shall he not with him also freely give us all things? Who shall lay anything to the charge of God's elect?

Who, indeed.

Romans 8:33-34. It is God that justifieth. Who is he that condemneth?

No one can, for: —

183

Romans 8:34. It is Christ that died,

And so put our sins to death.

Romans 8:34. Yea rather, that is risen again,

And so hath justified us.

Romans 8:34. Who is even at the right hand of God,

And so has carried us into heaven by his representing us there.

Romans 8:34. Who also maketh intercession for us.

Whose everlasting plea, therefore, silences all the accusations of the devil.

Romans 8:35. Who shall separate us from the love of Christ? shall tribulation, or distress or persecution, or famine, or nakedness or peril, or sword?

They have all been tried. In different ages of the world, the saints have undergone all these, and yet has never one of them been taken away from the love of Christ. They have not left off loving him, nor has he left off loving them. They have been tried, I say.

Romans 8:36. As it is written. For thy sake we are killed all the day long; we are accounted as sheep for the slaughter.

What is the result of it?

Romans 8:37-39. Nay, in all these things we are more than conquerors through him that loved us. For I am persuaded, that neither death, nor life, nor angels, nor principalities, nor powers, nor things present, nor things to come, nor height, nor depth, nor any other creature, shall be able to separate us from the love of God, which is in Christ Jesus our Lord.

Halleluiah! Blessed be his name.

This exposition consisted of readings from Psalms 138.; Isaiah 55:1-11; Romans 8:28-39.

ROMANS 9

Verses 1-5

Romans 9:1-3. I say the truth in Christ, I lie not, my conscience also bearing me witness in the Holy Ghost, That I have great heaviness and continual sorrow in my heart. For I could wish that myself were accursed from Christ for my brethren, my kinsmen according to the flesh:

The apostle is evidently about to make an extraordinary statement — a statement which would probably not be believed, and therefore, he gives as a preface the most solemn asseverations that are permitted to Christian men declaring that he is speaking the truth, and also that the Holy Ghost is bearing witness with his conscience that it is so — that he so loves the souls of his fellow-countrymen that, though the thing could never be, yet in a sort of ecstasy of love he could devote himself to anything so long as his countrymen might but be saved. "My kinsmen according to the flesh."

Romans 9:4-5. Who are Israelites; to whom pertaineth the adoption, and the glory, and the covenants, and the giving of the law, and the service of God, and the promises: Whose are the fathers, and of whom as concerning the flesh Christ came, who is over all, God blessed for ever. Amen.

The apostle never omits an opportunity of magnifying his Master. Though it did not seem to be called for by the immediate subject in hand yet he must put in a doxology to the name of Jesus. "Who is over all; God blessed for ever. Amen." How any believers in Scripture ever get to be disbelievers in the Deity of Christ is altogether astounding. If there is anything taught in the Word of God, it is assuredly that Paul comforts himself in a measure by the doctrine of election, which is fully spoken to in this chapter. My subject leads me to read again at the 10th chapter.

This exposition consisted of readings from Romans 9:1-5; and Romans 10.

Verses 1-25

The Jews thought that God must certainly save them. They thought they had a birth claim. Were they not the children of Abraham? Surely they had some right to it. This chapter battles the question of right. No man has any right to the grace of God. The terms are inconsistent. There can be no right to that which is free favor. We are all condemned criminals, and if pardoned, it must be as the result of pure mercy, absolute mercy, for desert there is none in any one of us.

Romans 9:1-2. I say the truth in Christ, I lie not, my conscience also bearing me witness in the Holy Ghost, That I have great heaviness and continual sorrow in my heart.

He never thought about his unbelieving brethren, without the deepest imaginable regret. How far is this from the spirit of those who look upon the ungodly without tears — settle it down as a matter that cannot be altered, and take it as a question of hard fate, but are never troubled about it. Not so the Apostle. He had great heaviness and continual sorrow in his heart.

Romans 9:3. For I could wish that myself were accursed from Christ for my brethren, my kinsmen according to the flesh:

He had just that self-sacrificing spirit of Moses, that he would lose anything and everything if they might but be saved. And this is the spirit which ought to actuate every Church of Christ. The Church that is always caring for her own maintenance is no church. The Church that would be willing to be destroyed if it could save the sons of men — which feels as if, whatever her shame or sorrow, it would be nothing if she could but save sinners — that Church is like the Lord, of whom we read, "He saved others: himself he could not save." Oh! blessed heart-break over sinful men, which makes men willing to lose everything if they might, but bless and win men to Christ! "My kinsmen," says he, "according to the flesh."

Romans 9:4-5. Who are Israelites; to whom pertaineth the adoption, and the glory, and the covenants, and the giving of the law, and the service of God, and the promises; Whose are the fathers, and of whom as concerning the flesh Christ came, who is over all, God blessed forever. Amen.

What dignity has God put upon ancient Israel! How favored far beyond any of us in these particulars! They had the light, when the rest of the world was in darkness. Theirs was the law, and theirs the covenant promises. Above all, of them it was, that Christ came. Our Saviour was a Jew. Forever must that race be had in respectful honour, and we must pray for their salvation.

Romans 9:6-7. Not as though the word of God hath taken none effect. For they are not all Israel, which are of Israel: Neither, because they are the seed of Abraham, are they all children: but, in Isaac shall thy seed be called.

Now, the Apostle is getting to his point. You Jews claim to have the mercy of God because you are of the seed of Abraham; but there is nothing in that, says he, for God made a distinct choice of Isaac to the rejection of Ishmael, as he did afterwards of Jacob, and then Esau was left out.

Romans 9:8. That is, thy flesh which are the children of the flesh, these are not the children of God: but the children of the promise are counted for the seed.

Now, Isaac was not the child of Abraham's flesh. He was born according to promise, when his mother was past age, and his father well stricken in years. His was the birth according to the promise, and that is the way the line of grace runs — not according to the flesh, but according to the promise. If, then, all my hope of heaven lies upon my being a child of godly parents, it is an Israelitish hope, and good for nothing. If my hope of heaven lies upon my having been born according to the promise of

God —born of his grace and of his power — in that line the covenant stands. God is determined that it shall be so.

Romans 9:9-13. For this is the word of promise. At this time will I come, and Sarah shall have a son. And not only this; but when Rebecca also had conceived by one, even by our father Isaac; (for the children being not yet born, neither having done any good or evil, that the purpose of God according to election might stand, not of works, but of him that calleth;) It was said unto her, The elder shall serve the younger. As it is written, Jacob have I loved, but Esau have I hated.

So, then, there is no claim of birth, for he that had the claim of birth, even Esau, is passed by. There is, indeed, no claim at all, for God gives freely, according to his own will, blessing the sons of men.

Romans 9:14. What shall we say then? Is there unrighteousness with God? God forbid.

There is no unrighteousness, in anything that he does: and in the winding up of all affairs, it shall be seen that God was righteous as well as gracious.

Romans 9:15-16. For he saith to Moses, I will have mercy on whom I will have mercy, and I will have compassion on whom I will have compassion. So then it is not or him that willeth, nor of him that runneth, but of God that showeth mercy.

That is where it must begin. When men are condemned, what can they appeal to, but the mercy of God? Where is the hope of men, but in the sovereignty of the Most High?

Romans 9:17-24. For the scripture saith unto Pharaoh, Even for this same purpose have I raised thee up, that I might show my power in thee, and that my name might be declared throughout all the earth. Therefore hath he mercy on whom he will have mercy, and whom he will he hardeneth. Thou wilt say then unto me, Why doth he yet find fault?

For who hath resisted his will? Nay but, O man, who art thou that repliest against God? Shall the thing formed say to him that formed it, Why hast thou made me thus? Hath not the potter power over the clay, of the same lump to make one vessel unto honour, and another unto dishonour? What if God, willing to show his wrath, and to make his power known, endured with much long-suffering the vessels of wrath fitted to destruction: And that he might make known the riches of his glory on the vessels of mercy, which he had afore prepared unto glory. Even us, whom he hath called, not of the Jews only, but also of the Gentiles?

There was the sting of it. They could not endure that God should in his divine sovereignty save Gentiles as well as Jews. But he has done so, and 'he has sent the Gospel to us; while they, having refused it, are left in the darkness which they chose.

Romans 9:25. As he saith also in Osee, I will call them my people, which were not my people; and her beloved, which was not beloved.

Oh! what a splendid verse is this! Let some here who have been far from God until now, and never had a gracious thought, nevertheless, hear what he has done and will do again. "I will call them my people, which were not my people; and her beloved which was not beloved."

This exposition consisted of readings from Exodus 3:1-14; Romans 9:1-25.

Verses 1-33

Paul begins by expressing his great sorrow because the Jews had rejected Christ.

Romans 9:1-3. I say the truth in Christ, I lie not, my conscience also bearing me witness in the Holy Ghost, That I have great heaviness and continual sorrow in my heart. For I could wish that myself were accursed from Christ for my brethren, my kinsmen according to the flesh:

They hated Paul intensely; nothing could surpass the malice of the Jews against the man whom they reckoned to be an apostate from the true faith, because he had become a follower of Christ, the Nazarene. Yet note what is Paul's feeling towards his cruel countrymen; he is willing, as it were, to put his own salvation in pawn if by doing so the Jews might but be saved. You must not measure these words by any hard grammatical rule, you must understand them as spoken out of the depths of great loving heart; and when such a heart as Paul had begins to talk, it speaks not according to the laws of logic, but according to its own immeasurable feelings. There were times when he almost thought that he would himself consent to be accursed, "anathema," cast away, separated from Christ, if thereby he could · save the house of Israel, so great was his love towards them. Of course, this could not be; and no one understood better than Paul did that there is only one Substitute and one Sacrifice for sinners. He only mentioned this wish to show how dearly he loved the Jews, so that on their account he had great heaviness and continual sorrow in his heart for his brethren, his kinsmen according to the flesh. Do you, dear friends, feel that same concern about your brethren, your kinsmen according to the flesh? If they are not saved, do you greatly wonder that they are not, if you have no such concern about them? But when once your heart is brought to this pitch of agony about their souls, you will soon see them saved.

Romans 9:4-5. Who are Israelites; to whom pertaineth the adoption, and the glory, and the covenants, and the giving of the law, and the service of God, and the promises; Wwhose are the fathers, and of whom as concerning the flesh Christ came, who is over all, God blessed for ever. Amen.

This was what troubled the apostle so much concerning the Jews, that they should have such extraordinary privileges, and yet should be cast away; most of all, that Jesus Christ, the Saviour of men, should be of their race, bone of their bone, flesh of their flesh, and yet they would not receive him, or be saved by him. Oh, the terrible hardness of the human heart; and what poor things the richest privileges are unless the grace of God goes with them to give us the inner secret of true faith in Christ!

Romans 9:6. Not as though the word of God hath taken none effect.

Paul is always jealous lest anyone should suppose that the Word of God has failed, or that the purpose of God has come to naught.

Romans 9:6-7. For they are not all Israel, which are of Israel: Neither, because they are the seed of Abraham, are they all children:

Now he goes on to show that the blessings of God's grace do not go according to carnal descent. It is true that God promised to bless the seed of Abraham, yet he meant that word "seed" in a very special sense.

Romans 9:7. But, In Isaac shall thy seed be called.

By passing over Ishmael, God showed that there was nothing of saving in blood or birth. Ishmael was the firstborn son of Abraham; but he was passed by, for the promise was, "In Isaac shall thy seed be called."

Romans 9:8-10. That is, They which are the children of the flesh, these are not the children of God: but the children of the promise are counted for the seed. For this is the word of promise, At this time will I come, and Sarah shall have a son. And not only this; but when Rebecca also had conceived by one, even by our father Isaac; —

When there were twins to be born of her; —

Romans 9:11-13. (For the children being not yet born, neither having done any good or evil, that the purpose of God according to election might stand, not of works, but of him that calleth;) It was said unto her, The elder shall serve the younger. As it is written, Jacob have I loved, but Esau have I hated.

Here were two children born at the same time; yet Esau was not of the true "seed." It matters not how closely you may be connected with the people of God, unless you have a new heart and a right spirit yourself, you still do not belong to the covenant seed, for it is not of the flesh that this privilege comes, but God has chosen a spiritual seed according to his own good pleasure.

Romans 9:14. What shall we say then? Is there unrighteousness with God? God forbid.

Paul knew very well that there would always be some who would cry out against this doctrine, that men would say that God was partial and unjust. If he had not foreseen that the declaration of this doctrine would provoke such remarks, he would not have put it so: "What shall we say then? Is there unrighteousness with God? God forbid."

Romans 9:15-16. For he saith to Moses, I will have mercy on whom I will have mercy, and I will have compassion on whom I will have compassion. So then it is not of him that willeth, nor of him that runneth, but of God that showeth mercy.

You know that the modern way of meeting objections to Scripture is to give up everything to the infidel, and then say that you have won him; but the true Christian way is to give up nothing at all, and if the truth is objectionable, to make it, if possible, still more objectionable, to turn the very hardest side it has right in front of the face of man, and to say, "This is God's truth; refuse it at your peril." I believe that half the attempts to win over unbelievers by toning down truth have simply been to the dishonouring of the truth and the destruction of the doubter, and that it would be always better to do as the apostle here does, — not to disavow the truth, but to proclaim it as fully, and faithfully, and plainly as possible. Let us again read what he here says: "Is there unrighteousness with God? God forbid. For he saith to Moses, I will have mercy on whom I will have mercy, and I will have compassion on whom I will have compassion. So then it is not of him that willeth, nor of him that runneth, but of God that showeth mercy."

Romans 9:17. For the scripture saith unto Pharaoh,

Paul is now going to show the other side of the same truth: "The scripture saith unto Pharaoh," —

Romans 9:17-19. Even for this same purpose have I raised thee up, that I might show my power in thee, and that my name might be declared throughout all the earth. Therefore hath he mercy on whom he will have mercy, and whom he will he hardeneth. Thou wilt say then unto me, Why doth he yet find fault? For who hath resisted his will?

Paul knew that the doctrine would be objected to on this ground; evidently he intended to assert something which was open to this objection, which would naturally suggest itself to men: "Why doth he yet find fault? For who hath resisted his will?

Romans 9:20-25. Nay but, O man, who art thou that repliest against God? Shall the thing formed say to him that formed it, Why hast thou made me thus? Hath not the potter power over the clay, of the same lump to make one vessel unto honour, and another unto dishonour? What if God, willing to show his wrath, and to make his power known, endured with much longsuffering the vessels of wrath fitted to destruction: And that he might make known the riches of his glory on the vessels of mercy, which he had afore prepared unto glory, Even us, whom he hath called, not of the Jews only, but also of the Gentiles? As he saith also in Osee, I will call them my people, which were not my people; and her beloved, which was not beloved.

See the grand style in which God talks to men. He speaks after a royal fashion: "I will." tie asks no man's leave for what he will do: "I will call them my people, which were not my people; and her beloved, which was not beloved."

Romans 9:26. And it shall come to pass, that in the place where it was said unto them, Ye are not my people; —

Though he himself had said it,-

Romans 9:26. There shall they be called the children of the living God.

See the splendor of this divine sovereignty, which shows itself in wondrous, unexpected acts of grace, selecting and taking to itself those who seem to be self-condemned, and even condemned by himself, of whom he had said, "Ye are not my people."

Romans 9:27-31. Esaias also crieth concerning Israel, Though the number of the children of Israel be as the sand of the sea, a remnant shall be saved: For he will finish the work, and cut it short in righteousness: because a short work will the Lord make upon the earth. And as Esaias said before, Except the Lord of Sabaoth had left us a seed, we had been as Sodoma, and been made like unto Gomorrha. What shall we say then? That the Gentiles, which followed not after righteousness, have attained to righteousness, even the righteousness which is of faith. But Israel, which followed after the law of righteousness, hath not attained to the law of righteousness.

Does it not seem strange that men who were outwardly sinful, who were utterly ignorant of any way of righteousness, and even indifferent to it, have been by the grace of God led to seek righteousness in the right way, namely, by faith in Christ, and they have found it, and God's electing love is seen in them; while others, who seem very sincere and devout as to outward ritual, by following it and it alone, have missed their way, and never found the true righteousness? The sovereignty of God appears in the choosing of those who follow the way of faith, and the casting away of those who follow the way of mere outward righteousness. But why did Israel miss the way?

Romans 9:32-33. Wherefore? Because they sought it not by faith, but as it were by the works of the law. For they stumbled at that stumblingstone; As it is written, Behold, I lay in Sion a stumblingstone and rock of offence:

I say again that there have been great attempts made, with logical dynamite, to blow up this great rock of offence, and to clear away every difficulty from the path of the man who wants to be saved by his own method, and to make everything pleasant all round for him; but against this course of action we bear our continual protest, for it is not according to the mind of God, or the teaching of his Word: "As it is written, Behold, I lay in Sion a stumblingstone and rock of offence."

Romans 9:33. And whosoever believeth on him shall not be ashamed.

But if they believe not on him, they shall one day be ashamed; and, meanwhile, the eternal purpose of God shall still stand, he shall still be glorious whatever men shall do, or shall not do.

Verses 26-32

The Jews thought that God must certainly save them. They thought they had a birth claim. Were they not the children of Abraham? Surely they had some right to it. This chapter battles the question of right. No man has any right to the grace of God. The terms are inconsistent. But that same grace delights to save and bless even the perverse and rebellious who will yield to its blessed power.

Romans 9:26. And it shall come to pass, that in the place where it was said unto them, ye are not my people; there shall they be called the children of the living God.

That In the very same place where their sins made it patent and palpable they were not God's people — in that very same place shall men confess that they are the children of the living God. Oh! what has not grace done?

Romans 9:27-29. Esaias also crieth concerning Israel, Though the number of the children of Israel be as the sand of the sea, a remnant shall be saved: For he will finish the work, and cut it short in righteousness: because a short work will the Lord make upon the earth. And as Esaias said before, Except the Lord of Sabaoth had left us a seed, we had been as Sodoma, and been made like unto Gomorrha.

God has a people, then, even in Israel with all its rejection; and he Always will have, for he will never make the seed of Abraham to be as Sodom and Gomorrha. He will love his own, and glorify himself in the midst of his people.

Romans 9:30. What shall we say then?

Why, say this: —

Romans 9:30. That the Gentiles, which followed not after righteousness, have attained to righteousness, even the righteousness which is of faith.

For thousands of years they worshipped brutish idols and blocks and stones. Their philosophy was mixed with filthiness. Their lives were abhorrent to God. Even these at last have attained to righteousness, even the righteousness which is by faith, for the Gospel being preached among the Gentiles, they have believed in Jesus, and they are saved.

Romans 9:31. But Israel, which followed after the law of righteousness, hath not attained to the law of righteousness.

Israel followed after the law of righteousness with many ceremonies and external washings, and wearings of phylacteries and bordered garments. Alas poor Israel

Romans 9:32. Wherefore? Because they sought it not by faith, but as it were by the works of the law. For they stumbled at that stumbling-stone;

And God is determined that they that are of the law shall not inherit it. He has made it a sovereign decree that the believer shall be justified and saved, and none else. They sought it not by faith, But as it were by the works of the law.

ROMANS 10

Verses 1-15

Romans 10:1. Brethren, my heart's desire and prayer to God for Israel is, that they might be saved.

Let this be our "heart's desire and prayer to God for Israel." Sorrows upon sorrows have come to the Lord's ancient people even down to this day; and they have been scattered and peeled, and rent and torn in almost every land. Who does not pity their griefs and woes? Let it be our heart's desire and daily prayer for Israel that they may be saved through faith in the Messiah whom they have so long rejected.

Romans 10:2. For I bear them record that they have a zeal of God, but not according to knowledge.

In Paul's day, they were most diligent in the observance of every form of outward devotion, and many of them sincerely desired to be right with God; but they did not know how to attain the desired end.

Romans 10:3. For they being ignorant of God's righteousness, and going about to establish their own righteousness, have not submitted themselves unto the righteousness of God.

Perhaps I am addressing some who are very anxious to be right with God; they are by no means hypocrites, but are really awakened to a sense of their danger, yet they cannot get peace of mind; and the reason is that, like the Israelites, they are "going about to establish their own righteousness." "Going about" — that is to say, struggling, striving, searching, worrying themselves to get a righteousness of their own which they never will obtain, and being ignorant of "the righteousness of God" which is completed in Christ, and which is freely bestowed upon all who believe in him. Alas! they "have not submitted themselves" unto this righteousness of God, and there is a kind of hidden meaning in the apostle's expression. They are so proud that they will not submit to be saved by the righteousness of another, even though that other is the

Lord Jesus Christ himself. Yet this is the main point, — the submission of our proud will to the righteousness of God.

Romans 10:4. For Christ is the end of the law for righteousness to everyone that believeth.

Christ is the ultimatum of the law; and when we go to the law, accepted and protected by him, we present to the law all that it can possibly demand of us. Christ has fulfilled the law on behalf of all who believe in him, so that its curse is abolished for all of us who approach it through Christ.

Romans 10:5-9. For Moses describeth the righteousness which is of the law, that the man which doeth those things shall live by them. But the righteousness which is of faith speaketh on this wise, Say not in thine heart, Who shall ascend into heaven? (that is, to bring Christ down from above:) or, Who shall descend into the deep? (that is, to bring up Christ again from the dead.) But what saith it? The word is nigh thee, even in thy mouth, and in thy heart: that is, the word of faith, which we preach; that if thou shalt confess with thy mouth the Lord Jesus, and shalt believe in thine heart that God hath raised him from the dead, thou shalt be saved.

"The righteousness which is of faith" is quite another thing from the righteousness which is of the law. It is not a thing of doing, and living by doing, but of trusting, and living for ever by trusting. What are you at, — you who would fain clamber up to the stars, or you who would plunge into the abyss? There is nothing for you to do, there is nothing for you to feel, there is nothing for you to be, in order that God may accept you; but, just as you are, if you will receive Christ into your heart, and confess him with your mouth, you shall be saved. Oh, this glorious way of the salvation of sinners, — so simple, yet so safe, — so plain, yet so sublime, — for me to lay aside my own righteousness, and just to take the righteousness of Christ, and be covered with it from head to foot! I may well be willing to lay aside my own righteousness, for it is a mass of filthy rags, fit only to be burned.

Romans 10:10-14. For with the heart man believeth unto righteousness; and with the mouth confession is made unto salvation. For the scripture saith, whosoever believeth on him shall not be ashamed. For there is no difference between the Jew and the Greek: for the same Lord over all is rich unto all that call upon him. For whosoever shall call upon the name of the Lord shall be saved. How then shall they call on him in whom they have not believed?

How can there be true prayer where there is no faith? How shall I truly pray to God if I do not really believe in him? "For he that cometh to God must believe that he is, and that he is a rewarder of them that diligently seek him."

Romans 10:14. And how shall they believe in him of whom they have not heard?

We must know what it is that we are to believe; and knowing it, we shall be helped by the Holy Spirit to believe it,

Romans 10:14. And how shall they hear without a preacher?

If the Word of the Lord does not get to a man either by the living voice, or by the printing-press, which often takes the preacher's place, how is he to believe it? You see here what I have often called "the whole machinery of salvation." First comes the preacher proclaiming the gospel, then comes the sinner listening to it, then comes the hearer believing it, and in consequence calling upon the name of the Lord as one who is saved with his everlasting salvation.

Romans 10:15. And how shall they preach, except they be sent?

Here is the great engine at the back of all the machinery, — God sending the preacher, — God blessing the Word, — God working faith in the heart of them that hear it.

Romans 10:15. As it is written, How beautiful are the feet of them that preach the gospel of peace, and bring glad tidings of good things?

Verses 1-19

Romans 10:1-3. Brethren, my heart's desire and prayer to God for Israel is, that they might be saved. For I bear them record that they have a zeal of God, but not according to knowledge. For they being ignorant of God's righteousness, and going about to establish their own righteousness, have not submitted themselves unto the righteousness of God.

A fault — a pitiable and grievous fault — that men should be in earnest and very zealous, and yet nothing should come of it, because they spend that zeal in a wrong direction. Men would make themselves righteous. They would come before God in the apparel of their own works, whereas God has made a righteousness already, which he freely gives, and for us to try and produce another is to enter into rivalry with God — to insult his Son, and do dishonour to his name. May God grant that any here who are very zealous in a wrong direction may receive light and knowledge, and henceforth turn their thoughts in the right way.

Romans 10:4-5. For Christ is the end of the law for righteousness to every one that believeth. For Moses describeth the righteousness which is of the law, That the man which doeth those things shall live by them.

That is the righteousness of the law. We are not under that covenant now. We shall never attain to righteousness that way.

Romans 10:6-9. But the righteousness which is of faith speaketh on this wise, Say not in thine heart, Who shall ascend into heaven? (that is, to bring Christ down from above:) Or, who shall descend into the deep? (that is, to bring up Christ again from the dead.) But what saith it? The word is nigh thee, even in thy mouth, and in thy heart: that is, the word of faith, which we preach; That if thou shalt confess with thy mouth the Lord Jesus, and shalt believe in thine heart that God hath raised him from the dead, thou shalt be saved.

How very simple! No climbing, no diving, no imagining, no long reckoning of the understanding, no strangling of the mental faculties. It is just believe God's testimony concerning his Son, and thou shalt be saved.

Romans 10:10-11. For with the heart man believeth unto righteousness; and with the mouth confession is made unto salvation. For the scripture saith, Whosoever believeth on him shall not be ashamed. For there is no difference between the Jew and the Greek:

[Gentile] in this matter.

Romans 10:12-13. For the same Lord over all is rich unto all that call upon him. For whosoever shall call upon the name of the Lord shall be saved.

This was the old prophecy of Joel. The Jews knew it. It is the new teaching of the gospel. The Gentiles know it. Oh! who would not wish to be in that broad "whosoever," that he might find salvation?

Romans 10:14-15. How then shall they call on him in whom they have not believed? and how shall they believe in him of whom they have not heard? and how shall they hear without a preacher! And how shall they preach, except they be sent? as it is written, How beautiful are the feet of them that preach the gospel of peace, and bring glad tidings of good things!

So that, rightly looked upon, the humblest preacher of the gospel stands in the most solemn relationship towards mankind. His Master sends him. He tells his message. Men hear it, believe it, and by it are saved. Happy is the messenger. Well may his heart rejoice, even when his soul is heavy, because he has such work to do in his Master's name.

Romans 10:16. But they have not all obeyed the gospel. For Esaias saith, Lord, who hath believed our report?

And what Isaiah says, many and many a preacher since has had to say. "Woe, woe to us for this."

Romans 10:17-19. So then faith cometh by hearing, and hearing by the word of God. But I say, Have they not heard? Yes, verily, their sound went into all the earth, and their words unto the ends of the world. But I say, Did not Israel know?

Did not the Jewish people have a time of hearing and instruction? Certainly they knew, and they knew also that the gospel was not to be confined to them. They had a warning that it should even be taken from them and sent to other nations.

This exposition consisted of readings from Isaiah 42:1-17; Isaiah 43:18-25; Romans 10:1-19.

Verses 1-20

Romans 10:1. Brethren, my heart's desire and prayer to God for Israel is, that they might be saved.

Now these people had persecuted the Apostle. Wherever he went they had followed him up; they had hindered his work: they had sought his life: and yet this was the only return that he made to them — to desire and pray that they might be saved. Let us never be turned aside from this loving desire for those among whom we dwell. We wish them nothing worse — we cannot wish them anything better than that they may be saved. Let us not only desire it, but let us pray for it. Let us turn our desires into the more practical and holy form of intercession.

Romans 10:2. For I bear them record that they have a zeal of God, but not according to knowledge.

Always make allowance for anything that is good in those who, as yet, are not converted. We must not be unjust with them because we desire to be faithful to them.

Romans 10:3. For they being ignorant of God's righteousness, and going about to establish their own righteousness, have not submitted themselves unto the righteousness of God.

And that is the great mischief with persons who are not saved. They are very sincere, very earnest, but they will not submit to the righteousness of God; they will not agree to be made righteous by the grace of God through Jesus Christ; but they "go about" — that is the Apostle's word. It is very expressive of the energy men will put into it, and the shifts to which they will have recourse, in order to work out a righteousness of their own. They will go about, aye, even to the very gates of hell; they will try to climb up by prayers, even to the gates of heaven. They will go about to establish their own righteousness, but they do not know the righteousness of God, and they refuse to submit themselves to it.

Romans 10:4. For Christ is the end of the law for righteousness to every one that believeth.

He that believes in Christ is as righteous as the law could have made him, if he had kept it perfectly. The end of the law is righteousness; that is, the fulfilling of it; and he that hath Christ will see the law fulfilled in Christ, and the righteousness of Christ applied to himself.

Romans 10:5-6. For Moses describeth the righteousness which is of the law, That the man which doeth those things shall live by them. But the righteousness which is of faith speaketh on this wise,

Ah! that is a very different sort of thing. It does not speak about doing and living, "but the righteousness which is of faith speaketh on this wise."

Romans 10:6-9. Say not in thine heart, Who shall ascend into heaven? (that is, to bring Christ down from above:) Or, Who shall descend into the deep? (that is, to bring up Christ again from the dead.) But what saith it? The word is nigh thee, even in thy mouth, and in thy heart: that is, the word of faith, which we preach; That if thou shalt confess with thy mouth the Lord Jesus, and shalt believe in thine heart that God hath raised him from the dead, thou shalt be saved.

There is the gospel in a nutshell. What a very simple way it is — to believe these great facts about the Lord Jesus Christ — really to believe them so that they become practical factors in your life. This is all the way of salvation. Christ has not to be fetched down. He has come. He has not to be fetched up. He has risen from the dead. The work is finished. What thou hast to do is to believe in that finished work and accept it as thine own, and thou shalt be saved.

Romans 10:10. For with the heart man believeth unto righteousness; and with the mouth confession is made unto salvation.

How different all this from that going about to establish our own righteousness, this setting up of prayers, and tears, and church-goings, and chapel-goings, and good works, and I know not what beside! Instead of that, here is Christ set forth, and "ye are complete in him." If you take him to be yours, you are "accepted in the Beloved," and "being justified by faith, you have peace with God through our Lord Jesus Christ." Oh! what a blessing is this!

Romans 10:11. For the scripture saith, Whosoever believeth on him shall not be ashamed.

Though he did much that he need be ashamed of, yet when the law so brought him to believe in Jesus Christ for righteousness, he is righteous, and he is so righteous that he shall never be ashamed of his righteousness, nor ashamed of his faith in Christ. Would God that some who are going about after a righteousness of their own would be led to try this method, and believe in Jesus Christ.

Romans 10:12. For there is no difference between the Jew and the Greek:

What a blessed word that is — "There is no difference between the Jew and the Gentile"! There are some that want to keep up that difference. They say that we are Israel, or something of the kind. I do not care what we are. There is no difference between the Jew and the Greek.

Romans 10:12. For the same Lord over all is rich unto all that call upon him.

Someone said to me, "I think that the Romish Church cannot be the Church of Christ. I do not think that the Church of England is the Church of Christ. Do you think the Baptists are the Church of Christ?' And my answer was, "The Church of Christ is to be found mixed up in all churches, and no churches at all." It is a people that God has chosen from among men, and they are to be found here and there and everywhere, a spiritual seed that God has marked out to be his own; and they are known by this —that they call upon the Lord, and "the same Lord over all is rich unto all that call upon him."

Romans 10:13. For whosoever shall call upon the name of the Lord shall be saved.

We call upon that name by having confidence in it; by speaking to God in prayer, using that name; by adoring and reverently proclaiming the majesty and the name of God. Whosoever shall call upon or invoke that great name shall be saved.

Romans 10:14. How then shall they call on him in whom they have not believed?

For at the bottom of the saving invocation or call there must be real faith. There cannot be any true worship of God unless it be grounded and bottomed upon faith in God.

Romans 10:14. And how shall they believe in him of whom they have not heard?

There cannot be such a thing as believing what has never been spoken in our hearing, and has never been made known to us. Of course, reading often answers the same end as hearing. It is a kind of hearing of the Word; but a man must know, or he cannot believe.

Romans 10:14. And how shall they hear without a preacher?

How is that possible? Do you see the machinery of the gospel? There is the calling upon the name. That comes of faith. There is the faith that comes of hearing; but there is the hearing that comes of preaching. Now a little farther.

Romans 10:15. And how shall they preach, except they be sent?

Poor preaching. It will not be the kind of preaching that produces believing hearing, except they be sent. If God does not send the man, he had better have stopped at home. It is only as God sends him that God will bless him. He is bound to back up his own messenger when he delivers God's own message. "How shall they preach, except they be sent?"

Romans 10:15. As it is written, How beautiful are the feet of them that preach the gospel of peace, and bring glad tidings of good things!

And they are so beautiful because, you see, God has put them at the root of everything. God makes the preacher whom he sends to be the source of so much good, or the channel of so much good, for by his preaching comes the hearing, and by the hearing comes the believing, and out of the believing come the calling upon the name and the salvation.

Romans 10:16. But they have not all obeyed the gospel.

"But." A sorrowful "but" is this. Oh! this is the mischief of it. The gospel, then, has an authority about it; or else the Apostle would not speak of obeying the gospel. Men are bound to believe what God declares to them, and their not believing is a disobedience. "They have not all obeyed the gospel."

Romans 10:16. For Esaias saith, Lord, who hath believed our report?

As if there were so few that did believe it, that he had to ask who they were.

Romans 10:17. So then faith cometh by hearing, and hearing by the word of God.

You are wise, therefore, dear friend, if you are seeking salvation to be a hearer of the Word; but mind that it is the Word of God that you hear, because the word of man cannot save you. It may delude you. It may give you a false peace; but the hearing that saves is hearing which comes by the Word of God. Oh! take care, then, that you do not run hither and thither just because of the cleverness of certain speakers; but keep you to the Word of God whoever preaches it, for "faith cometh by hearing, and hearing by the Word of God."

Romans 10:18. But I say, Have they not heard?

These very people for whom the Apostle prayed — have they not heard?

Romans 10:18. Yes verily, their sound went into all the earth, and their words unto the ends of the world.

The preaching of the gospel went forth amongst those Israelites, who rejected it. Wherever they went, the gospel seemed to follow them like their shadows. They could not escape from it, but they did not believe it.

Romans 10:19. But I say, Did not Israel know?

Assuredly, Israel did know, but did not believe.

Romans 10:19. First Moses saith, I will provoke you to jealousy by them that are no people, and by a foolish nation I will anger you.

Moses told them that it would be so if they rejected Christ. Christ would be preached to the Gentiles, and those whom they thought to be foolish would come in and accept what they had rejected.

Romans 10:20. But Esaias is very bold, and saith, I was found of them that sought me not; I was made manifest unto them that asked not after me.

He told them, therefore, that God would save a people who hitherto had never sought after God — that he would send the gospel to a people that were dead in sin, and had never asked to receive the light and life of God.

Verses 1-21

Romans 10:1. Brethren, my heart's desire and prayer to God for Israel is, that they might be saved.

Desire is the mother and the soul of prayer "my heart's desire and prayer." These Israelites had hunted Paul about, and sought to kill him. They were his deadly enemies; but the only return he made them was to pray that they might be saved. I hope you will never have a worse wish for your worst foe.

Romans 10:2. For I bear them record that they have a zeal of God, but not according to knowledge.

Always see all the good that is to be seen; and, when you have to reprove and rebuke begin by admitting what is good: "They have a zeal of God, but not according to knowledge."

Romans 10:3. For they being ignorant of God's righteousness, and going about to establish their own righteousness, have not submitted themselves unto the righteousness of God.

They were very zealous; but it was blind zeal. They were very energetic; but they used their energy in going the wrong way. God has a righteousness, and our wisest course is to submit to it. Our righteousness, if we set it up in opposition to God's way of salvation, will only increase our sin. You can be ruined by your righteousness, as surely as by your unrighteousness, if you set it in the place of salvation by grace through faith in Jesus Christ. "They being ignorant of God's righteousness, and going about to establish their own righteousness, have not submitted themselves unto the righteousness of God."

Romans 10:4. For Christ is the end of the law for righteousness to every one that believeth.

If we get Christ by believing, we have the righteousness of the law. All that ever could come to us by the highest and most perfect obedience to the law, we get by faith in Christ Jesus.

Romans 10:5. For Moses describeth the righteousness which is of the law,

And being the one through whom the law was given, he knew how to describe it; and we may be sure that he made no mistake. This is his description of legal righteousness: —

Romans 10:5. That the man which doeth those things shall live by them.

That is it: "Do and live." That is the law, and a very just law, too. Leave anything undone, or break the command in any respect and you die; that is the law.

Romans 10:6. But the righteousness which is of faith —

This is quite another thing; it —

Romans 10:6. Speaketh, on this wise,

And it is Moses who speaks here, as in the previous verse. This is what the righteousness of faith says: —

Romans 10:6-9. Say not in thine heart, Who shall ascend into heaven? (that is, to bring Christ down from above:) Or, Who shall descend into the deep? (that is, to bring up Christ again from the dead.) But what saith it? The word is nigh thee, even in thy mouth, and in thy heart: that is, the word of faith, which we preach; that if thou shalt confess with thy mouth the Lord Jesus, and shalt believe in thine heart that God hath raised him from the dead, thou shalt be saved.

God's way of salvation, then, is "Believe and live." Believe in Christ; Christ dying, Christ raised from the dead. If thou so believest, thou art saved. Thou needest not mount to heaven in rapture, nor dive to hell in remorse. As thou art, believe and live. This is the way of the righteousness of God.

Romans 10:10. For with the heart man believeth unto righteousness; and with the mouth confession is made unto salvation.

True faith must be accompanied by an open confession. Come forward, and outwardly own what you inwardly believe. Remember those words of the Lord Jesus, "He that believeth and is baptized shall be saved." Here, as there, the confession is put after the faith, as indeed it must be. First, the reality, the thing signified, faith; afterwards, the outward and visible sign in the confession of that faith.

Romans 10:11. For the scripture saith, Whosoever believeth on him shall not be ashamed.

He need never be ashamed of his faith. It will bear him up; it will bear him through; it will bear him up to heaven.

Romans 10:12-13. For there is no difference between the Jew and the Greek: for the same Lord over all is rich unto all that call upon him. For whosoever shall call upon the name of the Lord shall be saved.

That is it wonderful sentence; catch at it. Doubting, troubled spirits, catch at it, believe it, practice it; and you shall find it true.

Romans 10:14-15. How then shall they call on him in whom. they have not believed? and how shall they believe in him of whom they have not heard? and how shall they hear without a preacher? and how shall they preach, except they be sent? as it is written, How beautiful are the feet of them that preach the gospel of peace, and bring glad tidings of good things!

See here the whole machinery of salvation. God provides salvation in Christ Jesus, he sends the preacher to tell of it, men hear, they believe, and salvation is theirs. You have not to make it righteousness, you have to accept the one that is made for you. It is not what you shall do that shall save you; it is what Christ has done. You are to get out of self-confidence into confidence in him; and as soon as you do so, you are saved.

Romans 10:16. But they have not all obeyed the gospel.

Oh, no; all who have beard it, have not obeyed it! There are many here who have beard it from their childhood, and yet they have not obeyed it. Notice the word "obeyed", for the gospel comes to you with the force of a command. If you reject it, you sin against it, for it is your duty to accept it: "but they have not all obeyed the gospel."

Romans 10:16. For Esaias saith, Lord, who hath believed our report?

So few were the obedient, that he asked where they were.

Romans 10:17-18. So then faith cometh by hearing, and hearing by the word of God. But I say, Have they not heard?

Oh, may they hear, indeed!

Romans 10:18-19. Yes verily, their sound went into all the earth, and their words unto the ends of the world. But I say, Did not Israel know? First Moses saith, I will provoke you to jealousy by them that are no people, and by a foolish nation I will anger you.

Has he not done it? Israel is rejected, and remains without Christ, while many out of "a foolish nation" of Anglo-Saxons, who were idolaters, have accepted Christ. People who were regarded as dogs by God's chosen nation Israel have come into the house of the Lord, and still Israel refuses to come.

Romans 10:20. But Esaias is very bold, and saith, I was found of them that sought me not;

Hear, then, you who have never had any religion; you who seldom go to the house of God. Even you may be saved, for it is written, "I was found of them that sought me not."

Romans 10:20. I was made manifest unto them that asked not after me.

Here is the manifestation of sovereign grace, God choosing and saving whom he wills, irrespective of their condition; exercising the sovereignty of his mercy in saving the most undeserving.

Romans 10:21. But to Israel he saith, All day long I have stretched forth my hands —

In the attitude of invitation and entreaty, and readiness to receive, —

Romans 10:21. Unto a disobedient and gainsaying people.

And that is what he has done to thee, O then careless child of pious parents, then unregenerate hearer of the Word! All day long has he stood and stretched forth his hands unto a disobedient and gainsaying people. The Lord forgive all such, for Jesus' sake! Amen.

12

Verses 1-16

Romans 12:1. I beseech you therefore, brethren,

Paul is a calm reasoner. He is a bold starer of truth, but here he comes to pleading with us. I think that I see him lift the pen from the paper and look round upon us, as. with the accent of entreaty, he says, "I beseech you, therefore, brethren, by the mercies of God, by God's great mercy to you, his many mercies, his continued mercies." What stronger plea could the Apostle have? "I beseech you therefore, brethren, by the mercies of God."

Romans 12:1. By the mercies of God, that ye present your bodies a living sacrifice, holy, acceptable unto God, which is your reasonable service.

Though he beseeches you to do it, he claims a right to it. It is but your reasonable service. Do we need to be entreated to be reasonable? I am afraid that we do sometimes. And what are we to do? To present our bodies to God, not our souls alone, to make real, practical work of it. Let this flesh and blood in which your body dwells be presented unto God, not to be killed and to be a dead sacrifice, but to live and still to be a sacrifice, a living sacrifice unto God, holy and acceptable to him. This is reasonable. God help us to carry it out.

Romans 12:2. And be not conformed to this world:

Do not live as men of the world do. Do not follow the customs, the fashions, the principles of the world. "Be not conformed to this world."

Romans 12:2. But be ye transformed

It is not enough to be nonconformists. Be transformed ones, altogether changed into another form.

Romans 12:2. By the renewing of your mind, that ye may prove what is that good, and acceptable, and perfect, will of God.

It is by holy living, by consecrated bodies, that we are to prove the will of God. We cannot know it, we cannot practically work it out, except by a complete consecration unto God.

Romans 12:3. For I say, through the grace given unto me, to every man that is among you, not to think of himself more highly than he ought to think; but to think soberly, according as God hath dealt to every man the measure of faith.

Humility is sober thinking. Pride is drunken thinking. He that thinks more of himself than he should is so far intoxicated with conceit; but he that judges aright and is, therefore, humble, thinks soberly. God give us to be very sober in our thoughts of ourselves.

Romans 12:4-5. For as we have many members in one body, and all members have not the same office: So we, being many, are one body in Christ, and every one members one of another.

Hence the diversity. If the hand were made exactly like the foot, it would not be a tenth part as useful; and if the eye only had the same faculty as the ear, it would not be able to see, and the whole body would be a loser thereby. Do we begin to compare eyes, and ears, and feet, and hands, and say, "This is the better faculty"? No. They are each one needful. So do not compare yourselves among yourselves, for if you are in the body of Christ, you are each one needful, and the peculiarity which you possess, and the peculiarity which your brother possesses, have their place in the body corporate, and must be precious before God.

Romans 12:6-8. Having then gifts differing according to the grace that is given to us whether prophecy, let us prophesy according to the proportion of faith; Or ministry, let us wait on our ministering: or he that teacheth, on teaching; Or he that exhorteth on exhortation:

Keep to your own work; stand in your own niche. If you are only an exhorter, do not pretend to teach. If your work is ministry, and you cannot prophesy, do not attempt to do it. Every man in his own order.

Romans 12:8-9. He that giveth, let him do it with simplicity; he that ruleth, with diligence; he that sheweth mercy, with cheerfulness. Let love be without dissimulation.

Do not pretend to a love that you have not got. Do not lard your speech with "dear" this and "dear" that, when there is no love in your heart; and even if your heart be full of love, show it without spreading molasses over your talk, as some do. "Let love be without dissimulation."

Romans 12:9. Abhor that which is evil;

Be a good hater. Abhor that which is evil

Romans 12:9. Cleave to that which is good.

Stick to it. Hold it fast. Do not go an inch beyond it.

Romans 12:10. Be kindly affectioned one to another with brotherly love;

Hear this, ye members of the church. Endeavor to carry it out by a kindly courtesy and a real sympathy one with another. "Be kindly affectioned one to another with brotherly love."

Romans 12:10. In honour preferring one another;

Putting another before yourself, aspiring after the second place, rather than the first.

Romans 12:11. Not slothful in business;

A lazy man is no beauty anywhere.

Romans 12:11. Fervent in spirit;

Burn. Let your very soul get hot.

Romans 12:11-12. Serving the Lord; Rejoicing in hope;

When you have not anything else to rejoice in, rejoice in hope.

Romans 12:12. Patient in tribulation;

The word "tribulation" signifies threshing as with a flail. Be patient when the flail falls heavily.

Romans 12:12-13. Continuing instant in prayer; Distributing to the necessity of saints;

When you have told your own necessity to God, then help the necessities of those who come to you.

Romans 12:13-14. Given to hospitality. Bless them which persecute you: bless, and curse not.

A Christian man cursing is a very awkward spectacle. Even the Pope, when he takes to cursing, as at least the former one used to do very liberally, seems as if he could hardly be the vicar of God on earth. Our work is to bless the sons of men. "Bless and curse not."

Romans 12:15. Rejoice with them that do rejoice,

Do not be a wet blanket on their joys. If they have good cause for rejoicing, join in it. Help them to sing their hymn of gratitude.

Romans 12:15. And weep with them that weep.

Sympathize with mourners. Take a share of their burden. I really believe that it is easier to weep with them that weep than it is to rejoice with them that do rejoice; for this old flesh of ours begins to envy those who rejoice, whereas it does not so much object to sympathize with those that sorrow. Carry out both commands. "Rejoice with them that do rejoice. Weep with them that weep."

Romans 12:16. Be of the same mind one toward another.

Agree together, you Christian people. Do not be always arguing and discussing. Be of the same mind one towards another. In church life very much must depend upon our unity in mind as well as in heart. "One Lord, one faith, one baptism" — these help to make a good foundation for Christian fellowship.

ROMANS 15

Verses 1-16

Romans 15:1. We then that are strong ought to bear the infirmities of the weak, and not to please ourselves.

When we are free from scruples upon any point, and feel that there are things that we may do because we are strong, yet let us not do them if thereby we should grieve others who are weak. Let us think of their infirmities; and whatever liberty we may feel entitled to claim for ourselves, let us look at the matter from the standpoint of other people as well as from our Own, that we may bear the infirmities of the weak, and not seek to please ourselves.

Romans 15:2-3. Let every one of us please his neighbor for his good to edification. For even Christ—

Our Master, and Lord, and great Exemplar: "For even Christ"—

Romans 15:3. Pleased not himself; but, as it is written, The reproaches of them that reproached thee fell on, me.

He took the most trying place in the whole field of battle; he stood where the fray' was hottest. He did not seek to be among his disciples as a king is in the midst of his troops, guarded and protected in the time of strife; but he exposed himself to the fiercest part of all the conflict. What Jesus did, that should we who are his followers do, no one of us considering himself, and his own interests, but all of us considering our brethren and the cause of Christ in general.

Romans 15:4. For whatsoever things were written aforetime were written for our learning,—

This is as if somebody had said, "Why, Paul, it was David who said what you just quoted" "Yes," he replies, "I know that I quoted David, but he spoke in his own person concerning his Lord, 'for whatsoever things were written aforetime were written for our learning.'"

Romans 15:4-5. That we through patience and comfort of the scriptures might have hope. Now the God of patience and consolation—

"Comfort" is really the word he used, turning into prayer the thought which had been suggested by his use of the words "patience and comfort." "Now the God of patience and comfort"—

Romans 15:5. Grant you to be likeminded one toward another according to Christ Jesus:

"Make you to be unanimous, not concerning that which is evil, but that you may be of one mind in your likeness to Christ Jesus." What a blessed harmony it would be if, not only all in any one church, but all in the whole of the churches were likeminded one toward another according to Christ Jesus! It will be so when he gathers those who are now scattered; but may we never hope to have it so here on earth? I cannot tell; but, at any rate, let us all strive after it. Let us all endeavor to pitch our tune according to Christ's keynote; and the nearer we get to that, the less discord there will be in the psalmody of the church. We shall be likeminded with one another when we become likeminded with Christ; but not till then.

Romans 15:6-7. That ye may with one mind and one mouth glorify God, even the Father of our Lord Jesus Christ. Wherefore receive ye one another, as Christ also received us to the glory of God.

Christ did not receive us because we were perfect, because he could see no fault in us, or because he hoped to gain somewhat at our hands. Ah, no! but, in loving condescension covering our faults, and seeking our good, he welcomed us to his heart; so, in the same way, and with the same purpose, let us receive one another.

Romans 15:8. Now I say that Jesus Christ was a minister of the circumcision for the truth of God, to confirm the promises made unto the fathers:

228

It was to Abraham and his descendants that the promise was made that, in him, and in his seed, all the nations of the earth should be blessed. So our Lord came, as a Jew, to be "a minister of the circumcision." Let us never forget that he came to those whom we are apt to forget; and, peradventure, even to despise, "to confirm the promises made unto the fathers.'"

Romans 15:9-12. And that the Gentiles might glorify God for his mercy; as it is written, For this cause I will confess to thee among the Gentiles, and sing unto thy name. And again he saith, Rejoice, ye Gentiles, with his people. And again, Praise the Lord, all ye Gentiles; and laud him, all ye people. And again, Esaias saith, There shall be a root of Jesse, and he that shall rise to reign over the Gentiles; in him shall the Gentiles trust.

There were plain indications, in the Old Testament, that the blessing was meant for the Gentiles as well as for the Jews; but, still, it was made known to the Jews first, and we must never forget that.

Romans 15:13. Now the God of hope—

Turn back to the fourth verse, and note the expression, "that we through patience and comfort of the Scriptures might have hope;" then read in the fifth verse," The God of patience and comfort;" and see how Paul here goes back to that last word in the fourth verse, "Now the God of hope"—

Romans 15:13-16. Fill you with all joy and peace in believing, that ye may abound in hope, through the power of the Holy Ghost. And I myself also am persuaded of you, my brethren, that ye also are full of goodness, filled with all knowledge, able also to admonish one another. Nevertheless, brethren, I have written the more boldly unto you in some sort, as putting you in mind, because of the grace that is given to me of God. That I should be the minister of Jesus Christ to the Gentiles, ministering the gospel of God, that the offering up of the Gentiles might be acceptable, being sanctified by the Holy Ghost.

Now would have been the time for Paul to say that he had been made a minister "to offer the unbloody sacrifice of the mass," if such a thing had been right;—to offer up the daily sacrifice, as the so-called "priests" aver that, they now do; but he says nothing of the sort; and even when he represents the Gentiles as being offered up, he does not speak of any sacrifice going therewith, but says that it "might be acceptable, being sanctified by the Holy Ghost."

Verses 13-33

Romans 15:13-27. Now the God of hope fill you with all joy and peace in believing, that ye may abound in hope, through the power of the Holy Ghost. And I myself also am persuaded of you, my brethren, that ye also are full of goodness, filled with all knowledge, able also to admonish one another. Nevertheless, brethren, I have written the more boldly unto you in some sort, as putting you in mind, because of the grace that is given to me of God. That I should be the minister of Jesus Christ to the Gentiles, ministering the gospel of God, that the offering up of the Gentiles might be acceptable, being sanctified by the Holy Ghost. I have therefore whereof I may glory through Jesus Christ in those things which pertain to God. For I will not dare to speak of any of those things which Christ hath not wrought by me, to make the Gentiles obedient, by word and deed. Through mighty signs and wonders, by the power of the Spirit of God; so that from Jerusalem, and round about unto Illyricum, I have fully preached the gospel of Christ. Yea, so have I strived to preach the gospel, not where Christ was named, lest I should build upon another man's foundation: but as it is written, To whom he was not spoken of, they shall see: and they that have not heard shall understand. For which cause also I have been much hindered from coming to you. But now having no more place in these parts, and having a great desire these many years to come unto you; whensoever I take my journey into Spain, I will come to you: for I trust to see you in my journey, and to be brought on my way thitherward by you, if first I be somewhat filled with your company. But now I go unto Jerusalem to minister unto the saints. For it hath pleased them of Macedonia and Achaia to make a certain contribution for the poor saints which are at Jerusalem. It hath pleased them verily; and their debtors they are.

For these Achaians and Macedonians had received the gospel from the saints in Jerusalem. The Gentiles had been made partakers of their spiritual things, so it was their duty to minister to the poor Christian Jews in carnal things.

Romans 15:27-28. For if the Gentiles have been made partakers of their spiritual things, their duty is also to minister unto them in carnal things. When therefore I have performed this, and have sealed to them this fruit,-

That is, "when I have delivered the money, and obtained a receipt in full for it; when I have discharged my duty in this matter,"-

Romans 15:28-29. I will come by you into Spain. And I am sure that, when I come unto you, I shall come in the fullness of the blessing of the gospel of Christ.

He was sure of that, but he did not know how he would go in other respects. He did not know that he would go to Rome as a prisoner; he could not foresee that he would be sent there as an ambassador in bonds; and little, I wean, did he care in what manner he would go, so long as he had the absolute certainty that he should go "in the fullness of the blessing of the gospel of Christ."

Romans 15:30-31. Now I beseech you, brethren, for the Lord Jesus Christ's sake, and for the love of the Spirit, that ye strive together with me in your prayers to God for me; that I may be delivered from them that do not believe in Judaea; and that my service which I have for Jerusalem may be accepted of the saints;-

For there were some saints in Jerusalem who were very narrow-minded, and who hardly thought it right to accept anything from Gentiles. They had not got clear of their Jewish bonds, and Paul was a little afraid lest what he was taking to them might not be acceptable, so he asked the Romans to pray about that matter. Is there anything about which believers may not pray? If there be, then we have no right to have anything to do with it. Bring everything before God in prayer, for all right thing way lawfully be prayed about. So Paul asked the Christians in Rome to pray about that matter of his journey to Jerusalem, and also to pray for his return,-

Romans 15:32-33. That I may come unto you with joy by the will of God, and may with you be refreshed. Now the God of peace be with you all. Amen.

THANK YOU

Thank you for purchasing this book. We truly value your custom. This book was put together to provide you with a collection of good commentary resources on the books of the Bible. It is our prayerful hope that God might use this work for His own glory and sovereign will.

We would be delighted to hear from you and received any messages, suggestions or corrections. You can contact us at:

expansivecommentarycollection@gmail.com

It is our promise that you email address will not be added to any mailing list or used for any purpose other than to communicate regarding this commentary series.

We trust that the Lord will continue to bless you as you live for Him.

Made in the USA
Coppell, TX
17 June 2024

33605444R00134